RUDOLFO A. ANAYA

Critical Companions to Popular Contemporary Writers
Kathleen Gregory Klein, Series Editor

V. C. Andrews
  by E. D. Huntley

Maya Angelou
  by Mary Jane Lupton

Tom Clancy
  by Helen S. Garson

Mary Higgins Clark
  by Linda C. Pelzer

Arthur C. Clarke
  by Robin Anne Reid

James Clavell
  by Gina Macdonald

Pat Conroy
  by Landon C. Burns

Robin Cook
  by Lorena Laura Stookey

Michael Crichton
  by Elizabeth A. Trembley

Howard Fast
  by Andrew Macdonald

Ken Follett
  by Richard C. Turner

Ernest J. Gaines
  by Karen Carmean

John Grisham
  by Mary Beth Pringle

James Herriot
  by Michael J. Rossi

Tony Hillerman
  by John M. Reilly

John Irving
  by Josie P. Campbell

John Jakes
  by Mary Ellen Jones

Jamaica Kincaid
  by Lizabeth Paravisini-Gebert

Stephen King
  by Sharon A. Russell

Barbara Kingsolver
  by Mary Jean DeMarr

Dean Koontz
  by Joan G. Kotker

Robert Ludlum
  by Gina Macdonald

Anne McCaffrey
  by Robin Roberts

Colleen McCullough
  by Mary Jean DeMarr

James A. Michener
  by Marilyn S. Severson

Toni Morrison
  by Missy Dehn Kubitschek

Anne Rice
  by Jennifer Smith

Tom Robbins
  *by Catherine E. Hoyser and
  Lorena Laura Stookey*

John Saul
  by Paul Bail

Erich Segal
  by Linda C. Pelzer

Amy Tan
  by E. D. Huntley

Anne Tyler
  by Paul Bail

Leon Uris
  by Kathleen Shine Cain

Gore Vidal
  by Susan Baker and Curtis S. Gibson

RUDOLFO A. ANAYA

A Critical Companion

Margarite Fernández Olmos

CRITICAL COMPANIONS TO POPULAR CONTEMPORARY WRITERS
Kathleen Gregory Klein, Series Editor

Greenwood Press
Westport, Connecticut • London

Library of Congress Cataloging-in-Publication Data

Fernández Olmos, Margarite.
  Rudolfo A. Anaya : a critical companion / Margarite Fernández
Olmos.
    p.   cm.—(Critical companions to popular contemporary
writers, ISSN 1082-4979)
  Includes bibliographical references and index.
  ISBN 0-313-30641-9 (alk. paper)
  1. Anaya, Rudolfo A.—Criticism and interpretation. 2. Mexican
Americans in literature. 3. New Mexico—In literature. I. Title.
II. Series.
PS3551.N27Z8 1999
813'.54—dc21   99-17843

British Library Cataloguing in Publication Data is available.

Library of Congress Catalog Card Number: 99-17843
ISBN: 0-313-30641-9
ISSN: 1082-4979

First published in 1999

Greenwood Press, 88 Post Road West, Westport, CT 06881
An imprint of Greenwood Publishing Group, Inc.
www.greenwood.com

Printed in the United States of America

The paper used in this book complies with the
Permanent Paper Standard issued by the National
Information Standards Organization (Z39.48-1984).

10 9 8 7 6 5 4 3 2 1

To my sister, Jeannie,
for a lifetime of loving support

Contents

viii   <u>Contents</u>

Series Foreword

The authors who appear in the series Critical Companions to Popular Contemporary Writers are all best-selling writers. They do not simply have one successful novel, but a string of them. Fans, critics, and specialist readers eagerly anticipate their next book. For some, high cash advances and breakthrough sales figures are automatic; movie deals often follow. Some writers become household names, recognized by almost everyone.

But, their novels are read one by one. Each reader chooses to start and, more importantly, to finish a book because of what she or he finds there. The real test of a novel is in the satisfaction its readers experience. This series acknowledges the extraordinary involvement of readers and writers in creating a best-seller.

The authors included in this series were chosen by an Advisory Board composed of high school English teachers and high school and public librarians. They ranked a list of best-selling writers according to their popularity among different groups of readers. For the first series, writers in the top-ranked group who had received no book-length, academic, literary analysis (or none in at least the past ten years) were chosen. Because of this selection method, Critical Companions to Popular Contemporary Writers meets a need that is being addressed nowhere else. The success of these volumes as reported by reviewers, librarians, and teachers led to an expansion of the series mandate to include some writers with wide critical attention—Toni Morrison, John Irving, and Maya Angelou, for example—to extend the usefulness of the series.

The volumes in the series are written by scholars with particular expertise in analyzing popular fiction. These specialists add an academic focus to the popular success that these writers already enjoy.

The series is designed to appeal to a wide range of readers. The general reading public will find explanations for the appeal of these well-known writers. Fans will find biographical and fictional questions answered. Students will find literary analysis, discussions of fictional genres, carefully organized introductions to new ways of reading the novels, and bibliographies for additional research. Whether browsing through the book for pleasure or using it for an assignment, readers will find that the most recent novels of the authors are included.

Each volume begins with a biographical chapter drawing on published information, autobiographies or memoirs, prior interviews, and, in some cases, interviews given especially for this series. A chapter on literary history and genres describes how the author's work fits into a larger literary context. The following chapters analyze the writer's most important, most popular, and most recent novels in detail. Each chapter focuses on one or more novels. This approach, suggested by the Advisory Board as the most useful to student research, allows for an in-depth analysis of the writer's fiction. Close and careful readings with numerous examples show readers exactly how the novels work. These chapters are organized around three central elements: plot development (how the story line moves forward), character development (what the reader knows of the important figures), and theme (the significant ideas of the novel). Chapters may also include sections on generic conventions (how the novel is similar or different from others in its same category of science, fantasy, thriller, etc.), narrative point of view (who tells the story and how), symbols and literary language, and historical or social context. Each chapter ends with an "alternative reading" of the novel. The volume concludes with a primary and secondary bibliography, including reviews.

The alternative readings are a unique feature of this series. By demonstrating a particular way of reading each novel, they provide a clear example of how a specific perspective can reveal important aspects of the book. In the alternative reading sections, one contemporary literary theory—way of reading, such as feminist criticism, Marxism, new historicism, deconstruction, or Jungian psychological critique—is defined in brief, easily comprehensible language. That definition is then applied to the novel to highlight specific features that might go unnoticed or be understood differently in a more general reading. Each volume defines two or three specific theories, making them part of the reader's understanding of how diverse meanings may be constructed from a single novel.

Taken collectively, the volumes in the Critical Companions to Popular Contemporary Writers series provide a wide-ranging investigation of the complexities of current best-selling fiction. By treating these novels seriously as both literary works and publishing successes, the series demonstrates the potential of popular literature in contemporary culture.

Kathleen Gregory Klein
Southern Connecticut State University

Acknowledgments

This book owes its existence to the loving help of friends and family. I am extremely grateful for the willing and proficient research assistance of Angela Spellman and Heidi Holder at Brooklyn College and for the patient support of my husband, Enrique, and my daughter, Gabriela. *Gracias a todos.*

1

The Life of Rudolfo A. Anaya

Rudolfo A. Anaya, the celebrated Mexican-American novelist, poet, play-wright, and essayist, has described his writing as a quest to "compose the Chicano* worldview—the synthesis that shows our true *mestizo*** identity—and clarify it for my community and for myself.... Writing for me is a way of knowledge, and what I find illuminates my life" (Clark, "Rudolfo Anaya" 42). His search for illumination led Anaya in 1972 to publish one of the most memorable works of Chicano fiction, *Bless Me, Ultima*. With this novel and the works that would follow, Anaya has also accomplished the formidable task of inscribing the physical and spiritual landscape of Chicano culture onto the terrain of contemporary U.S. literature.

EARLY YEARS: THE ORAL TRADITION

Rudolfo Anaya was born on October 30, 1937, in Pastura, a small village in the eastern *llanos*, or plains, of New Mexico, a barren, desolate

---

*"Chicano" refers to Mexican Americans born in the United States. The term was popularized in the 1960s.
**Mestizo* is a Spanish word that refers to persons of mixed European (Spanish) and indigenous ancestry.

area of mournful winds and tough vegetation that materializes in many of his writings. Landscape and a particular sense of place figure prominently in Anaya's novels. He has described Pastura and New Mexico in general as an area with which he feels a spiritual bond: "I don't believe a person can be born and raised in the Southwest and not be affected by the land. The landscape changes the man, and the man becomes his landscape" ("Writer's Landscape" 99).

Anaya's family life and his cultural community also had a profound impact on his first novel, which, as in the case of many authors, parallels details of the author's autobiography. "In *Bless Me, Ultima* . . . I looked at my childhood through the eyes of a novelist. . . . I explored childhood experiences, dreams, folklore, mythology, and communal relationships that shaped me in my formative years. Writing became a process of self-exploration" ("La Llorona" 417). His roots in the region run deep: Anaya's ancestors were among the original settlers of the land grant in Albuquerque called "La Merced de Atrisco" in the Rio Grande valley. In the mid-nineteenth century the family moved eastward into an area well suited for sheep and cattle grazing. The cultural richness of one of the oldest communities of the Americas informs Anaya's literary worldview. "My roots were planted here four hundred years ago when the Spaniard first came to the Southwest, and before that they were nourished by the pre-Columbian thought and cultures of the indigenous peoples, the native Americans" ("Writer's Sense of Place" 98).

Within the Hispanic community, Anaya's mother and father represented contrasting cultures—farmers and ranchers. Rafaelita Mares was the daughter of a farmer from the Puerto de Luna valley, a small village along the Pecos River south of the town of Santa Rosa. Her family grew crops and raised pigs, sheep, and cows. Poor, hardworking people and devout Catholics, they lived a traditional, settled life tied to their land. Rafaelita's first husband, in contrast, was a *vaquero* (cowboy), a man who preferred to ride horses and work with cattle rather than settle the land. Left a widow with two children after her husband's accidental death, Anaya's mother remarried a man from the area who also worked the cattle and sheep of the big ranchers, Martín Anaya. Together their family included Rudolfo, two additional sons (Anaya's older brothers, the "models for my manhood," left home as adolescents to fight in World War II), and four sisters. Anaya grew up in their company as well as that of the many visitors to his home—family members and friends, including the other vaqueros, who were larger-than-life figures for the young boy and who would now and then disrupt the silence of the llano by getting drunk with Anaya's father and shooting their pistols into the quiet nights of the plains.

When Anaya was still a small child his family moved to Santa Rosa, which was the social hub of the surrounding rural communities at the time. Located on Highway 66, the town represented for Anaya the link between the East and the West. Its proximity to the Pecos River provided the young boy with yet another opportunity for his evolving spiritual kinship with nature. Anaya passed much of his time there playing, hunting, and fishing with other boys. The river, he has stated, "haunted" him with its beautiful golden carp and its powerful "soul" or "presence," an energy similar to what he had earlier experienced on the plains. The forces of nature competed for the young boy's spirit with the religious instructions imparted by his mother and the parish priest. Rafaelita encouraged her son toward a life in the priesthood, while his father, a broken man tormented by a settled life in town away from the open plains he loved, rebelled silently. Anaya absorbed his mother's spirituality along with his father's skepticism; both combined to produce questions in the young boy's inquisitive mind.

Among Anaya's childhood recollections are the warmth of a loving home and his mother's evocative tales. He was told, for example, that he had been born with his umbilical cord tied around his neck. La Grande (the old wise one) was there to help in the delivery. The name of La Grande haunted the young boy's memory. As was the case with many women in traditional communities, she was not only a midwife but also a *curandera* (which has several meanings, among them, folk healer, shaman, and wise woman) who used the power of nature to cure illness. The author's imagination in later years would recall this woman and assign her even greater powers in the life of his first novel's young protagonist.

Anaya's mother also told him the story of the "choices" he had made as an infant. Symbolic items were placed around him—a saddle, a pencil, paper—and he supposedly crawled toward the implements of writing in lieu of those of his father's lifestyle.

These stories were complemented by the ancient legends that were told to all young Hispanic children, such as that of La Llorona, the wailing woman, a frightful tortured spirit who was said to have murdered her own children and could be heard crying for them in the night. The oral tradition, the "ancestral voices" of the people credited by Anaya with instructing him that there are signs in life "we must learn to interpret" ("Autobiography" 16), merged in the young boy with the stories he imbibed from the extended family that frequented his home. This rich cultural legacy—the simple family tales, anecdotes, sayings, and legends—and his early profound contact with the natural world around him represented Anaya's initial apprenticeship as a writer; to this he attributes his "instinct for storytelling" (Colby, *World Authors* 11).

SCHOOLING: THE WRITTEN TRADITION

In Santa Rosa Rudolfo Anaya attended school and moved into the world of English. He has described the experience as "shocking," adding that although he survived with the help of teachers, many of his classmates did not. The transition from the world of Spanish to the Anglo or English-speaking world proved difficult for many people of the community, including his own family. "My parents never quite made the adjustment. That pragmatic challenge was left to my generation" (Colby, *World Authors* 11).

Anaya's early years had been spent in a Spanish-speaking environment; he spoke Spanish exclusively as a child until the age of six. His early schooling—despite his love for learning—was a "difficult journey." This was perhaps made even more so by his first awareness of ethnic difference. Anaya's school years also represented his initial prolonged proximity with Anglo society. It was his first contact with the ideas of prejudice that would separate Anglos and Mexicans, a process the young boy did not yet understand. "I had always known that I was brown, that I was *mejicano* in the language of my community, that we were poor people. But those had been elements of pride, and now something had come to separate us" ("Autobiography" 19).

At the age of fifteen Anaya faced a new challenge. As was the case with many Hispanic families responding to social and economic changes after World War II, the Anayas joined the growing urban population of New Mexico, moving to Albuquerque, to the *barrio*, or neighborhood, of Barelas. He describes the city in the early 1950s as a "great place to be." Postwar Albuquerque was experiencing a boom, and life was secure, provided, of course, one kept to the areas considered "safe." Anaya's older brother knew the neighborhood and was respected there, thus affording the young teenager protection from the gangs and other urban ills that surrounded him. Anaya re-creates the trauma of the transition from rural to urban life for the Hispanic families of the times in his second novel, *Heart of Aztlán* (1976). He learned to negotiate city life and survive the streets while living the typical adolescent life of the era, from the "bebop dances in the gym" to "pretending we were cool as Jimmy Dean" ("Autobiography" 19). An event occurred, however, that would change the "rhythms of the soul" and alter his life forever.

On a warm, beautiful day he headed with his friends for a spot they had frequented many times before. An irrigation ditch provided the youths with a deep pool, and Anaya was the first to dive in. Then, he recalls, "the world disappeared." Having fractured two vertebrae in his neck, Anaya was instantly paralyzed and barely escaped drowning but for the help of a friend who realized what was happening. While Anaya has been reluctant to speak of this experience, he later wrote about it from a fictional perspective in the novel *Tortuga* (1979). There his extended stay at the Carrie Tingley Hospital, the dreadful anxiety, and the painful, determined months of recuperation become the ordeals of the young protagonist. Like the young man in the novel (the protagonist is nicknamed "Tortuga," or "Turtle," because his body is encased in a shell-like cast), Anaya had to "build a new faith inside the shell of bones and muscle" ("Autobiography" 20). *Tortuga* is the third novel of the initial trilogy of Anaya's works, all of which are linked not only by similar styles and themes but also by autobiographical details.

Despite the time spent in the hospital and his slow recuperation, Anaya managed to graduate on time from Albuquerque High School in 1956. Reflecting on his high school and college training, he has often commented that the school system of the time neglected the cultural reality of his Mexican-American heritage. Nowhere in the education he received could he find himself, his people, or the long and vital history of the Hispanic presence in the United States. After two unfulfilling years in business school, Anaya attended the University of New Mexico, majoring in English. He worked at several jobs to pay expenses and encountered many of the same difficulties he had met in high school: he felt unprepared to compete in an Anglo environment that "tolerated" Mexican Americans rather than encouraging them.

What sustained him during those years was the solidarity of fellow Chicano students. Few of his former barrio chums attended the university; the limited number of Chicanos who did attend supported one another, forming a clique to survive. They shared an interest in art and reading and critiqued one another's works. Anaya describes this as a time of intense literary activity during which he read extensively on literature, philosophy, and religion and made his first artistic endeavors in the genre of poetry. He discovered, however, that he "probably didn't have the gift that some people are blessed with" (Bruce-Novoa, *Chicano Authors* 186) and switched to narrative. While still at the University of New Mexico Anaya wrote several novels, some quite extensive, which he later destroyed. He refers to these attempts as "exercises in learning to write." In 1963 he graduated with a B.A. degree in English and American literature. In 1968 he completed an M.A. in English and earned another M.A. degree four years later in guidance and counseling, while supporting himself as a high school teacher. Except for brief trips to New York and other areas of the country, most of his life was spent in New Mexico. In 1966 he married Patricia Lawless, who is originally from Kansas and is also trained in guidance and counseling. He describes their ongoing relationship as having provided the stability and encouragement he needed as an artist, and he credits her for her constructive criticism of his writing. In the early 1960s he also began working on the story that would eventually become *Bless Me, Ultima*.

A MEETING WITH ULTIMA

Already well versed in the classics—Shakespeare, Dante, Milton, Pope—and in such poets as Walt Whitman, Dylan Thomas, T. S. Eliot, Ezra Pound, and Wallace Stevens, Anaya had also studied the writings of such contemporary American novelists as Ernest Hemingway, William Faulkner, John Steinbeck, and Thomas Wolfe. He was well acquainted with the myths and symbols of the legendary court of King Arthur, a metaphor Anaya uses in his essay "An American Chicano in King Arthur's Court" for the communal memory of Anglo Americans whose history and culture have been almost exclusively associated with "American" identity. Theirs was the culture he had been schooled in, but it could not serve to express the American reality of his particular heritage. From the Anglo-American novelists Anaya had learned about style and technique, but the voice he was searching for, the worldview he wished to discover in literature, was not to be found in those works nor in any others of the time. "I felt very much alone as a writer . . . Chicano writers 20 years ago were composing the first models and aesthetics of what would be Chicano literature" (González, "Songlines" 3). Anaya would have to discover on his own his creative voice as an author and that of his Hispanic/Indian/New Mexican identity.

In later years Anaya described his "meeting" with Ultima, the fictional character of his first novel, as a type of spiritual or magical encounter.

He had begun to work on the story of a young boy, Antonio Márez, and his relationship with his family. The story, however, never seemed to coalesce. He found it difficult to uncover the symbols and patterns of his own culture. The pathway to that process, he claims, was opened up to him by Ultima's "appearance." "That strong, old curandera . . . came to me one night and pointed the way. That is, she came to me from my subconscious, a guide and mentor who was to lead me into the world of my native American experience. Write what you know . . . learn who you really are" ("An American Chicano" 115). From that moment on, the ideas for the novel flowed as Anaya rediscovered the collective symbols of his Hispanic, indigenous heritage. Despite this burst of creative energy, however, Anaya struggled with the art of fiction writing. His painstaking attention to detail and the quest for a unique literary voice led Anaya to spend a total of seven years, from 1963 to 1970, to complete the novel. He wrote incessantly, producing at least seven complete drafts of the work before finally discovering his own expansive, evocative style.

Finding a publisher for the work, though, did not prove an easy task. Anaya attempted the traditional route of approaching mainstream publishers in New York and Boston; but the publishing world was not prepared in the 1970s for such nontraditional writers, particularly those expressing a bilingual, bicultural reality. Anaya was among the first to successfully incorporate Chicano culture's distinctive bilingualism in prose, but the mainstream publishing world was not interested. "For us, living in a bilingual world, it was very normal to allow Spanish into a story written in English—it's a process that reflects our spoken language—but [in approaching mainstream publishers] I was always called on it" (Clark, "Rudolfo Anaya" 42).

Rejection letters daunted neither Anaya's enthusiasm nor his faith in his novel. He continued to search for a publisher and found one purely by chance. In 1971, while reading a literary journal, *El Grito*, one of the first such Chicano publications founded by students, professors, and writers in California, Anaya noted a call for manuscripts. He promptly sent in his work, and the response was overwhelming: *Bless Me, Ultima* was awarded the Premio Quinto Sol in 1971 as the best novel written by a Chicano, and the work was published the following year by Quinto Sol Publishers. As a small press, Quinto Sol had the flexibility and the foresight to support fledgling authors. Their faith in Anaya proved to be well-founded.

Bless Me, Ultima was enthusiastically accepted by the Mexican-American community, the readers of which recognized themselves, their neighbors, and their friends in its characters. Word spread of the novel, which had emerged in a timely manner. The publication of the novel coincided with the burgeoning Chicano movement for social, economic, and political change, an outgrowth of the civil rights movement of the 1960s. The work struck a chord in the Mexican-American people, who were demanding cultural recognition along with their other concerns. It began to be taught in the newly created Chicano studies classes in colleges and universities and eventually reached a greater U.S. and international readership. Today is it considered one of very few Chicano "best-sellers." *Bless Me, Ultima* established Anaya's reputation as an author and as one of the founders of the contemporary Chicano literary movement. His works have been studied more than those of any other Chicano writer to date.

(RE)-CREATING MYTHS

By the time Anaya had published his second novel, *Heart of Aztlán*, in 1976, he was no longer a high school teacher. In 1974 the English Department at the University of New Mexico invited him to become a member of the creative writing faculty. Prior to this time Anaya and his wife had begun to spend time in Taos, New Mexico, where Anaya explored his Native-American roots. With his friends in the Taos Pueblo he learned the secrets of deer hunting, the ceremonial aspects of which, he claims, border on the "sacred." He and his wife also initiated their travels to Mexico, a place they would return to often, where Anaya came into personal contact with pre-Columbian (belonging to the time before the arrival of Christopher Columbus to America) cultures. While visiting Aztec and Mayan ruins he experienced the powerful spiritual components of these ancient civilizations. Their mysteries intrigued Anaya, who has described his frequent journeys to Mexico as visits to "renew" himself in his "spiritual homeland" ("Autobiography" 26).

Although the Anaya family no longer had any relatives living in Mexico, the author discovered deep personal affinities to Mexican culture through the Aztec myths, legends, and symbols that became important elements not only of his own novels but also of the Chicano movement of his time. Chicano activists were refashioning many of these myths to respond to their contemporary needs. One of these was the myth of the legendary land of "Aztlán" in the southwestern United States, where, it was believed, the Aztec peoples had originated. Thus Aztlán, or the U.S.

Southwest, came to be considered the spiritual birthplace and homeland of the Chicano people. The myth of Aztlán became a rallying call for Chicano political unity, but it also helped to construct the theme of *Heart of Aztlán*, which explores the relationship between people and the land and the disruption in the lives of internal migrants from the communal villages to the cities. "It was the infusion of myth into my work that surprised readers, I think. Our modern impulse had been working to hide our nature as mythmaking animals. I didn't, but instead I followed my intuition, the secrets whispered in the cells, as the source of illuminations. At that source you find humanity, you find myth" (Kenyon, "Visit" 126).

His novels from the 1980s are even more closely inspired by symbolism and mythology. *The Legend of La Llorona* (1984) is the fictionalized life of La Malinche, the interpreter/consort of the sixteenth-century Spanish conqueror of Mexico, Hernán Cortés; Anaya identifies her in the novel with the legendary weeping woman of ancient myth, La Llorona. *Lord of the Dawn: The Legend of Quetzalcóatl* (1987) presents the pre-Columbian Toltec deity as a redeemer and savior who walks among mankind bringing wisdom and art to humanity.

A trip to China with his wife in 1984, sponsored by a W. F. Kellogg Foundation fellowship, contributed to Anaya's evolving self-definition as a "New World" man. He refers to this experience in his travel journal, *A Chicano in China* (1986), as having helped him to identify more closely with that part of himself that is Native American (given the Asiatic origins of the indigenous people of the Americas): "I became a Chicano Chinaman" (Jussawalla and Dasenbrock, *Interviews* 246). Throughout his collections of short stories, children's tales, plays, and numerous essays, Anaya consistently emphasizes the significance of his diverse cultural heritage.

Once asked if, given the success of his first novel, which is still his best known, Anaya had found it difficult to move beyond *Bless Me, Ultima* and get on with other writing, the author dismissed the notion immediately. *Bless Me, Ultima* was a "blessing" that often comes only once in a lifetime, affording him the opportunity to explore other avenues and pursue his myriad interests. Rather than regret the fact that his most celebrated work was his very first, he is proud and pleased with his legacy: "I'm damned glad I have a *Bless Me, Ultima* at the middle passage of my life. I can pay attention to a lot of other things I want to write about. That's a very comfortable place to be" (González, "Songlines" 3).

The years following the publication of *Bless Me, Ultima* have been prolific for Rudolfo Anaya. As his novel's fame increased, so too the invitations to lecture in the United States and abroad and to serve in prestigious positions on editorial boards and foundation panels. These activities competed for his time with his teaching obligations and his disciplined and steady creative and scholarly writing. As a result, Anaya retired from teaching in 1993. He remains in Albuquerque, living with Patricia in the adobe home they designed high on the mesa west of the city, where he continues to write as well as encourage the development and direction of young artists, assuming the role of "elder" author with a genuine sense of responsibility. Cognizant of the fact that *Bless Me, Ultima* paved the way for the current boom in Chicano writing and publishing, Anaya has been active and generous in promoting other writers through his anthology collections and as editor of the literary journal *The Blue Mesa Review*. He describes these activities as "giving back part of my good fortune to the writing community" (González, "Songlines" 18). Despite the fact that his recent novels are being published by a major commercial publisher (Warner Books), providing him access to a broader public, he is still an active supporter and defender of small, nontraditional publishers, an institution he credits with having promoted the writings of serious though unknown authors who would have been otherwise ignored by mainstream publishing houses.

Anaya considers his departure from university teaching less a retirement than a "mid-career change," a "shift of energy into new areas" (González, "Songlines" 3). This change of direction has also been evident in the focus of his recent fiction. In 1992 Rudolfo Anaya published *Alburquerque*, the recipient of a PEN-West Fiction Award, a suspenseful story of a young boxer's quest for his family origins. The following two novels, *Zia Summer* (1995) and *Rio Grande Fall* (1996), represent Anaya's first incursion into the genre of detective fiction and a dramatic change in subject matter and style. Anaya's latest novel, *Shaman Winter* (1999), sends detective Sonny Baca into battle in dreams with his nemesis, Raven, the villain, who, unable to destroy him in the present, schemes to eliminate his ancient past. *Zia Summer* and *Rio Grande Fall* share with *Alburquerque* a focus on an urban environment, reflecting contemporary demographic realities. Less mystical and lyrical than his earlier novels, though more accessible, Anaya's recent novels explore sociopolitical, ethical, and environmental problems that result from power struggles inherent in rapid economic growth and development. *Jalamanta*, his novel published in 1996, described as a "New Age *Joshua*" (*Library Journal* 64), is the tale of a spiritual leader banished from the "Seventh City" who returns with wise teachings and challenging beliefs. While not directly related to his suspense/detective novels initiated by *Alburquerque*, *Jalamanta* nonetheless reflects the quest for truth that pervades all of Anaya's writings.

In this sense, therefore, Anaya's writings in the 1990s do not represent a complete break from his former literary or philosophical concerns. In many ways his focus has been consistent throughout his career: the setting of his major novels continues to be his beloved New Mexico, and the mysteries that must be solved by his new set of fictional characters draw them on spiritual quests for truths that are ancient and mystical even as they are modern and real. "We can still use the old myths of this hemisphere to shed light on our contemporary problems" ("Mythical Dimensions" 350). Rudolfo Anaya is still on a quest for illumination for himself and others, still clarifying his ever-evolving identity as a Chicano author. "We must tell who we are and define ourselves as a people, define our humanity . . . otherwise, someone else will do it and get it all wrong" (*Anaya Reader* xvii).

2

Rudolfo A. Anaya and the Chicano Literary Tradition

In a 1980 interview, Rudolfo Anaya reflected on the idea of the existence of a "distinctive perspective" within Chicano writing: "All literature, and certainly Chicano literature, reflects, in its more formal aspects, the mythos of the people, and the writings speak to the underlying philosophical assumptions which form the particular worldview of a culture." By "formal aspects" Anaya is not simply referring to style and technique but, rather, to an author's perspective, which should be "guided by culture, history, language, native mythology" (Bruce-Novoa, *Chicano Authors* 195). This sense of an author's moral responsibility, of social and cultural commitment, is not unique to Chicano literature, of course, but it does reflect its early origins in the United States. Rudolfo Anaya's writings, and *Bless Me, Ultima* in particular, have played an important role in the development of the Chicano literary movement, which has deep historical roots in U.S. culture.

U.S. HISPANIC CULTURE

In the century prior to the appearance of writing in English by inhabitants of what would become the United States of America, Spanish explorers and missionaries were already recording their own tales. The most famous of these, *La Relación* (The Account), was published in 1542 by Alvar Núñez Cabeza de Vaca. It describes his astounding adventures as a shipwreck survivor off the Texan coast and the eight years that he and three other explorers spent traveling in search of the Christian settlements in the Southwest. Along his journey, bereft of everything, he was taken captive by the Amerindians and found it necessary to reinvent himself, even becoming a faith healer in order to survive. The experience transformed Cabeza de Vaca; his appearance was so altered that when he finally encountered other Spaniards he was neither recognized nor believed. The American experience had converted Cabeza de Vaca into a hybrid, neither European nor Indian. Thus he is claimed today as a precursor and symbol of the cultural adaptation and transformation of Chicano culture that has also distinguished itself from both Mexican and U.S. Anglo society.

Recent studies of American literature have begun to recognize the writings in Spanish of such early Hispanic figures, as well as the oral tradition of tales, songs, poetry, and myths, as a rightful component of the U.S. literary tradition. In the years following the Mexican-American War and the Treaty of Guadalupe Hidalgo in 1848 (which forced Mexico to cede almost one-third of its territory, thereby giving control of Texas and most of present-day New Mexico, Arizona, and California to the Anglo north), writing by Mexican Americans appeared in Spanish and in English, including the first novel written by a Mexican American, *The Squatter and the Don* (1885) by María Amparo Ruiz de Burton. From the mid-nineteenth century through the early twentieth, the pressures of Anglo cultural domination would be resisted in Spanish-speaking communities in multiple local and regional publications that are still in the process of being recovered and reevaluated today.

CONTEMPORARY CHICANO LITERATURE

Genres and Themes

The first half of the twentieth century can be considered a period of ethnic consolidation in which the various Spanish-speaking groups in the United States—Mexicans, Cubans, Puerto Ricans—created economic, educational, and political organizations to defend their communities against racial and ethnic oppression. The fruit of their extensive efforts would ripen in the 1960s when the dramatic experiences and daily struggles of Latino people were brought into national focus as they joined with African Americans, Native Americans, and other minority groups to demand that their voices be heard. The Chicano movement emerged from the civil rights movement of the era, uniting Mexican Americans from all areas of the United States under a general banner of "La Raza" ("The People") and a specific identity—Chicano.

The catalyst for the Chicano political movement was the United Farm Workers strike against grape growers in 1965 led by César Chávez. Student and community organizers followed, often inspired by activist writers whose works promoted political struggles and served as a stimulus for action against social injustices. While some critics date the beginning of Chicano literature from the period following the Mexican-American War, most consider it a twentieth-century phenomenon, evolving from the Chicano civil rights struggles in the 1960s. The term "Chicano" came into popularity in this period, generally regarded as deriving from the sixteenth-century pronunciation of "Mexicano" ("Mechicano"). The ethnic awareness inspired by the Chicano political movement paved the way for a literary movement that developed its own themes and linguistic innovations.

The literature that emerged from Chicano *barrios*, or urban neighborhoods, played a vital role in the affirmation of roots and the articulation of values in direct contrast and opposition to U.S. Anglo culture. Autobiographical narrative—memoirs (personal accounts of memorable experiences), coming-of-age stories, and novels—dominated thematically to counterbalance mainstream images of youth and family life. The tension usually centered on the drive toward becoming "Americanized" versus loyalty to one's ethnic group. Other common themes include dislocation and migration, the hardships of barrio life, and the struggle for personal and communal identity. Drawing on centuries-old traditions, Chicano authors also constructed new myths to counter those of the larger society, such as the promotion of the mythological Aztlán, the legendary ancestral home of the Aztecs in the U.S. Southwest, which became a symbol of Chicano cultural origins, unity, and self-determination.

Language

One of the more original characteristics of contemporary Chicano literature (and of U.S. Latino writing in general) is in the area of linguistic innovation and experimentation. Many Chicano authors write in standard English, although a significant number create in Spanish or in a combination of English and Spanish (poets and playwrights in particular). Referred to linguistically as "code-switching" (or deprecatingly as "Spanglish"), the process involves combining languages in a manner that reflects the spoken idiom of millions of Chicanos. This linguistic variation, however, does more than simply reproduce Chicano linguistic modes; in the hands of a skilled author it can become a highly creative technique, revealing multiple levels of meaning and creating new expressive forms.

BLESS ME, ULTIMA AND THE EARLY NOVELS

Genres and Themes

Rudolfo Anaya has written works in many categories of literature throughout his career, both fiction and nonfiction. Among his fictional works—primarily his novels—Anaya has also explored several genres that treat his favorite themes or subjects in different ways. His earlier novels, for example, focus on the maturation and development of young male protagonists, or main characters. Later works emphasize mythological subjects; and his most recent novels delve into the genre of detective fiction.

It is helpful to be aware that Anaya considers his first three novels a trilogy, and, indeed, though loosely tied, they do share several significant similarities: (1) the central importance of a young male protagonist; (2) the reappearance of specific characters, as well as the repetition of certain types of characters (seers, mentors, shamanic figures); (3) the frequent use of symbols (objects that stand for something else) related to the natural world; and (4) similar geographic settings (New Mexico and the U.S. Southwest). The novels introduce characters that will reappear in later works conforming Anaya's fictional world and establishing themes to which Anaya will return throughout his career: the need to be in harmony with the natural world and the significance of tradition, myth, spirituality, and cultural identity as a means of healing and growth for the individual and the community.

Bildungsroman

Bless Me, Ultima, the first novel of the trilogy, has been described as the quintessential Chicano "bildungsroman," or coming-of-age novel.

The traditional bildungsroman follows the psychological development of a young child, narrating events from the protagonist's perspective. The character passes through the stages and conflicts an individual experiences on the road to maturity and integration into the wider society. Some famous examples of this genre in literature include Charles Dickens's *David Copperfield* (1850), Gustave Flaubert's *L'Education Sentimentale* (1869), James Joyce's *A Portrait of the Artist as a Young Man* (1916), and Thomas Mann's *The Magic Mountain* (1924) (considered an influence on Anaya's *Tortuga*). In *Bless Me, Ultima*, as in other works of this genre, the reader observes the process of the maturation of the main character through a series of rites of passage that affect the hero profoundly. In Anaya's novel the passage of time is limited to the main character's experiences from ages six to eight, much briefer than in the traditional bildungsroman. Young Antonio Márez learns much in those two years, however, thanks to his apprenticeship with the old folk healer who guides his growing consciousness.

Writers like Rudolfo Anaya from ethnically and racially marginalized groups in the United States take full advantage of the genre's potential. Often the coming-of-age novel as expressed in their works reflects the identity and adjustment problems of the protagonist in terms of the dominant cultural society. The novel reveals the influence of objective cultural values on the moral maturation of the central character. In asserting an identity not always condoned or accepted by the power structure of his or her society, the ethnic or minority writer attempts to create new standards and perspectives from their position on the periphery—far from the center—of mainstream society.

Bless Me, Ultima blazed a path within the Chicano literary tradition in the category referred to as "novels of identity" in which the main characters must redefine themselves within the larger society from the vantage point of their own distinct ethnicity. In identity novels the character is always aware of his or her cultural heritage (often questioning it as well) and attempts to forge some type of reconciliation with the larger society while maintaining a distinct identity. In *Bless Me, Ultima* the figure of Ultima in this context is crucial. As young Antonio's guide and mentor, her teachings not only bring him into contact with a mystical, primordial world but also with a culture—his own Hispanic/Indian culture—that he must learn to appreciate if he is ever to truly understand himself and his place within society.

The young Jason Chávez is a central character in *Heart of Aztlán*. He appeared in *Bless Me, Ultima* as the friend who had introduced Antonio to a mystical world of nature. In *Heart of Aztlán* Jason witnesses the

struggle and disintegration of his family in their new urban surroundings. As in Anaya's earlier novel, visionary characters point the way
toward the future; in *Heart of Aztlán* it is a blind old man named Crispín,
a poet/seer who plays a magical blue guitar. *Heart of Aztlán* differs significantly in style and theme from *Bless Me, Ultima*, however. Less lyrical
than Anaya's previous work, *Heart of Aztlán* is not strictly a coming-of-
age novel. Its main concern is Jason's family—in particular his father,
Clemente Chávez, whose manhood is tested in his harsh new environment—and the sociopolitical issues of social exploitation and abuse. The
fact that Anaya has referred to his first three novels as a "New Mexico
trilogy" can lead to the perception of the main characters of the three
works as forming a composite or combined protagonist: Antonio (*Bless
Me, Ultima*), Jason and Clemente (*Heart of Aztlán*), and the titular protagonist of *Tortuga* taken together would therefore represent different stages
of the composite character's development.

Tortuga, the third novel of the trilogy, returns to the motif (a recurring
theme or pattern) of rites of passage found in *Bless Me, Ultima*, but now
the main character is a paralytic sixteen-year-old boy, Tortuga. The autobiographical elements that are present in Anaya's first two novels also
characterize *Tortuga* (see chapter 1 herein), which traces the young man's
emotional and psychological growth as he heals both body and spirit.
His spiritual journey ends in his physical recovery and in the discovery
of his destiny: he will become an artist who sings the truth about his
people. Once again Anaya's novels are united by recurring characters:
Tortuga's instrument is the magical blue guitar left to him by Crispín of
Heart of Aztlán, so that the boy will "take his turn." *Tortuga*, which won
the Before Columbus American Book Award in 1979, is more successful
than *Heart of Aztlán* in blending the mythic and the realistic, and it returns to the lyrical, poetic tone of *Bless Me, Ultima*.

Setting

Anaya's earliest memories as a boy growing up in rural New Mexico
had a profound impact on his writing (see chapter 1). He has often commented on the influence of nature and landscape on his creative sensi-
bility: the landscape of the Southwest is described by Anaya as a power
that touched his "primal memory," allowing him to discover the "essential symbols" of his writing. Setting is therefore more than simply a

point of reference: "place, imagination and memory . . . are inextricably wound together in my work" ("Writer's Landscape" 98).

Anaya has expressed a spiritual kinship with the majestic environment of his region of the United States; nature, for Anaya, creates an "epiphany," an enlightenment or illumination, that he believes can produce profound changes in those who are open to being a part of it. He credits his ability to respond to *la tierra* (the land) to the elders of his community, who taught him to be conscious of and in harmony with his environment: "When the entire sense of the landscape—characters, emotion, experience, detail and story—permeates [the writer's] craft, the reader will respond, and that response is the beginning of a new epiphany" ("Writer's Landscape" 102).

Myths and Archetypes

In addition to the unity of setting (all three novels take place in New Mexico), the inclusion of autobiographical details, and the repetition of several characters and mystical motifs, the novels of Anaya's initial trilogy also share his affinity for dream sequences and archetypal figures. Critics have found it useful to refer to the theories of psychiatrist Carl G. Jung regarding myths, archetypes, and a collective unconscious in understanding Anaya's use of dream sequences, particularly in *Bless Me, Ultima* and *Tortuga*.

A myth can be defined as a tale that portrays in symbolic language the origins of a culture. Classical myths are legendary or traditional stories that were created and passed down by generations to explain how natural phenomena came into existence or how human activity originated. Occasionally they embody deeper concepts and human feelings. The ancient poets and writers were born into cultures with established mythologies or collections of such tales; Anglo writers have both recurred to those ancient established mythologies and, though less frequently, created their own. The poet William Blake, for example, felt the need to create his own mythological system, combining elements of Christianity with his own spiritual ideas and those of other cultures. D. H. Lawrence blended elements of Christianity with the pre-Columbian myth of the deity Quetzalcóatl as material for his novel *The Plumed Serpent* (1926). Some authors strive for a universal myth that will embody the experiences of all human beings. The novel *Moby-Dick* (1851) by Herman Melville, for example, is referred to as a myth precisely because it symbolizes a primal conflict—the struggle between man and the forces of nature—that stems from an idea universal to all people. For Jung the stuff of myth lies in what he called the "collective unconscious" of the human race.

The Swiss psychiatrist Carl Gustav Jung (1875–1961) was a student of Sigmund Freud and his theories regarding the unconscious broadened those of his mentor. Jung demonstrated close parallels between ancient myths and psychotic fantasies; human motivation, he felt, had to be understood in terms of a larger creative energy. In *Psychology of the Unconscious* (1912) he proposed the idea that the unconscious is composed of two dimensions: the personal, which would include the mental and material life of the individual, and the collective unconscious, inherited feelings, thoughts, and memories shared by members of a culture or universally by all humans. The collective unconscious is made up of what Jung called "archetypes," or primordial images that appear in dreams and fantasies. These primordial images might find expression in characteristic forms—the divine child, the Earth Mother, the wise old man, and so forth—that are frequently the themes of religion, fairy tales, and mythologies.

Some of these archetypes make their way into Rudolfo Anaya's frequent dream sequences and mythic symbols. In *Bless Me, Ultima* and *Tortuga* in particular, dreams reveal crucial stages in the internal evolution of the characters; they are woven into the framework of all three novels of the trilogy. Anaya's novels were also among the initial Chicano writings that recaptured a sacred mythic vision from pre-Columbian (dating to before Columbus's arrival in America), pre-Christian traditions and successfully incorporated this worldview into contemporary fiction. Precisely this mythic quality of *Bless Me, Ultima*, however, is what led to some of its most strident criticism.

Although universally praised for its unique story and subtle beauty, it should be recalled that *Bless Me, Ultima* was first published during a very politicized era in U.S. society; thus a political critique of the novel soon surfaced. Detractors, usually Marxist critics, observed that the work lacked a bold political message and concentrated instead on less important themes of myth and symbolism. Specifically, they felt that the focus of progressive Chicano literature should be critical analysis of capitalism and the ways in which that economic system exploits the working class. Anaya's novel, they claim, reverts to an illusory and romanticized vision of the past rather than pressing for social change in the present. What have been perceived by some as the work's shortcomings are perceived by others as its strengths. Many believe that *Bless Me, Ultima* transcends the narrow perceptions of what has been characterized as "ethnic" or "regionalist" literature and is a timeless tale that goes beyond a strictly Mexican-American experience to reflect a more universal experience, thereby becoming Anaya's most enduring legacy to American letters.

FROM MYTH TO MYSTERY: THE QUEST CONTINUES

In the years between the appearance of *Tortuga* and his next full-length novel, *Alburquerque* (1992), Rudolfo Anaya ventured into other literary genres. *The Silence of the Llano* (1982), his collection of short stories, continues to examine themes that characterize his earlier works: mythmaking, the power of language and writing, dreams, and human nature. In addition he has produced children's stories, plays, travel journals, and numerous scholarly essays, many of which are collected in *The Anaya Reader* (1995).

Anaya's fascination with primeval antiquity and myth did not end with the initial trilogy of novels. Two novellas (short prose narratives) explore these themes directly. *The Legend of La Llorona* (1984) combines history and folklore in a fictionalized life of La Malinche (Doña Marina), the Aztec interpreter/consort of the Spanish conquistador Hernán Cortés. The novella draws parallels between this fascinating woman—perceived by many as a Mexican "Eve" or traitor to her people and by others as a tragic victim of her times—and the legendary figure of La Llorona, a frightening villainous figure in many Hispanic childhood myths. *Lord of the Dawn: The Legend of Quetzalcóatl* (1987) also returns to legend and myth, rewriting the tale of the Toltec deity Quetzalcóatl, who has been associated in pre-Columbian culture with agriculture, the arts, and spirituality.

Furthermore, *Jalamanta* (1996), fashioned in the tradition of these earlier works, may have a main character who is an original contemporary creation, but the tone of the work is that of an earlier, ancient time. Jalamanta is a spiritual leader who, despite great opposition and repression, teaches the meaning of love. Reviewers have described the character as a "kind of Christic guru preaching an exotic blend of ego psychology, Christian theology and Hinduism" (*Library Journal* 64). Clearly Anaya believes that a contemporary readership can benefit from ancient and enduring truths and lessons.

Rudolfo Anaya's novels in recent years are a departure in genre and style, although in many respects they retain characteristics of his first three. *Alburquerque* reflects a new emphasis on contemporary social issues that directly affect the U.S. Southwest region and a new literary focus: mystery and suspense. The main character, a young boxer named Abrán González, is on a quest to discover his personal identity as he searches for his Mexican father. The issue of origins permeates this work, extending to the very name of the city of Albuquerque, which lost its original spelling (restored by Anaya in the title) as a result of Anglo domination of the area (an Anglo stationmaster in the nineteenth century, we are told, found it more convenient to drop the "r"). A real estate development scheme to divert the Rio Grande and create a commercial atmosphere that will threaten the traditional way of life of the Hispanic and Indian communities is a subplot of the novel, which includes the magical scenes and characters typical of Anaya's works. *Alburquerque* has been described as a "magical book that heals like the hands of a *curandera* shaman" (*Review of Contemporary Fiction* 201).

Zia Summer (1995) introduces a new character into the Anaya cast, the private detective Sonny Baca (who appears briefly in *Alburquerque*), a man who by profession must probe for the truth but whose search leads to greater discoveries regarding his racial and regional history and that of his ancestors. He must solve the murder of his cousin, whose body had been drained of blood and etched with the ancient Zia sun symbol by a terrorist group. The story contains elements of New Age cults and ancient rituals combined with political corruption and environmental activism. In *Rio Grande Fall* (1996) Sonny becomes a shamanic character himself, joining the cast of wise teachers and seers that began with Ultima. The mysteries he will encounter can once again be solved with ancient wisdom.

Anaya's first incursions into the detective/mystery genre, *Zia Summer* and *Rio Grande Fall*, follow the traditional conventions of detective fiction: an apparently insoluble crime must be solved by an individual (often an amateur) by means of logic and deductive reasoning. The author carefully reveals clues that must be detected by a sharp-witted sleuth (and also by the reader who attempts to match his or her wits with the central character's) in order to arrive at a solution to the problem. The detective story was initiated by Edgar Allan Poe in his "Murders in the Rue Morgue" (1841) and has evolved over the years into a myriad of types and categories. In modern fiction the detective genre usually emphasizes the psychological implications or the violent nature of the crimes, but the larger conventions of the genre remain basically the same.

Having chosen this genre for his recent works, Anaya's detective novels nevertheless continue to explore his ongoing themes regarding the U.S. Southwest and his cultural and spiritual concerns. The setting is still his magical New Mexico, the cultural tensions focus on the communities he knows best—Hispanics and Anglos—and the stress remains on the blending of ancient traditions with modern transformations. The innovation of a Chicano detective whose investigations draw him into a world of clashing, overlapping cultures and unexpected spiritual dimensions is a novelty within U.S. Latino writing and helps pave the way for others.

In *Shaman Winter* (1999) Sonny Baca returns to do battle with the villain encountered in *Zia Summer*, the *brujo* (sorcerer) Raven, an enemy from past lives, who, like Sonny, is an "old soul." Raven and Sonny are the latest shamanic-type characters in a long list of Anaya fictional healers and visionaries. The author Tony Hillerman, famed for his original detective fiction with Native-American protagonists, has referred to Rudolfo Anaya as the "godfather and guru of Chicano literature." Many undoubtedly would agree.

Bless Me, Ultima
(1972)

In Rudolfo Anaya's first novel he turned to his life experiences for inspiration. The story of the awakening of the consciousness of a young boy growing up in a small New Mexico town shortly after World War II closely parallels the author's own life (see chapter 1 herein). At the same time, however, *Bless Me, Ultima* is a highly original work with a unique story and a universal appeal that established Anaya's international reputation. This chapter will focus on his best-known novel, a work of poetic beauty and richness that introduces the themes and motifs that have become the hallmark of Anaya's writing.

NARRATIVE STRATEGIES

How can a story told from the vantage point of a seven-year-old boy express profound insights and complex ideas? *Bless Me, Ultima* accomplishes the task by being an extended flashback—that is, by assuring the reader from the very beginning that the events described, although seemingly occurring in the present, in fact occurred at an earlier time. The narrator is, therefore, by implication, an adult. Anaya is able to maneuver this tension of the older implied narrator and the younger voice of the child-protagonist Antonio Márez by carefully re-creating the reactions of a small boy. Antonio's comments reflect the expected limitations of a child of that age. For Antonio, World War II is a "far-off war of the Japanese and the Germans," for example, and other historical events are explained in an equally simple, age-appropriate manner.

The reader is informed that Ultima, a respected midwife, came to stay with Antonio Márez and his family the summer that he was almost seven years old. Her arrival marks a beginning—"the beginning that came with Ultima" (1)—and, indeed, Antonio's story begins and ends with her. Subsequent references in the same chapter to a time "long after Ultima was gone and I had grown to be a man" (13) affirm the fact that, although the story is presented in the voice of a young boy, the events are actually those of a remembered youth. Time and chronology assume additional significance; time is described as "magical," it "stands still" and is linked with the character of Ultima. She represents origins and beginnings. Her very name implies extremes and the extent of time and distance that Antonio will travel on his passage from innocence into awareness.

Bless Me, Ultima is an accessible novel despite its grounding in Chicano folk culture and myth and its occasional use of Spanish. It follows a linear, or straightforward, story development, a plotline that is clearly defined, and avoids the more experimental prose styles of other writers. Levels of narration are delineated for the reader by the use of italics, a device Anaya employs frequently. Antonio's dream sequences, for example, are separated from the rest of the narration by italics, indicating a different dimension of consciousness. The first chapter serves important functions in plot development and structure. It gently guides the reader toward essential story elements such as setting, characters, and historical background, and it introduces the major conflicts that will form the basis for the dramatic tension throughout the novel. The technique of foreshadowing, which can often provide structural and thematic unity to a work, first appears in the introductory chapter.

"Foreshadowing" refers to the device of hinting at events to come; later events are therefore prepared for or shadowed forth beforehand, building suspense and reader expectation. In *Bless Me, Ultima* foreshadowing ranges from statements that openly indicate future events to symbolic premonitions in dreams that suggest them. After Antonio's home is described in Chapter One as a place that offers the young boy a unique vantage point from which to observe family incidents, he refers to the tragedy of the sheriff's murder that has yet to occur, the anguish of his brothers' future rebellion against their father, and the many nights when he will see Ultima returning from her moonlit labors gathering the herbs that are a folk healer's remedies. Ultima, who rarely speaks and whose words are therefore significant, states that "there will be something" between herself and Antonio, suggesting a strong and important relationship yet to come. But the most effective foreshadowing technique is found in Antonio's dream sequences throughout the novel, the first of which occurs in Chapter One. These sequences express the dread and anxiety of his inner world but are also frequently premonitions of the future. Antonio's dreams provide both a structural and thematic framework for the novel as they illustrate past events and suggest future conflicts.

SETTING

The setting is of particular importance in this novel, as it is in most of Anaya's fiction. Nature is part of the magic that will teach young Antonio that seemingly incarnate elements are actually living beings, whose beauty and value the young boy will discover with Ultima's help—a river that sings, land that impresses its mysteries into the narrator's "living blood" (1). The setting, the world of nature in rural New Mexico, assumes a significance similar to that of a character in terms of its influence on people and events. Since setting is of paramount importance in so much of Anaya's work, the landscape, the environment, the forces of nature, the *llano* (plains) of New Mexico all combine to create a powerful sense of place that produces an experience Anaya has referred to as an "epiphany," a sudden flash of enlightenment or a revealing intuition often occasioned by something trivial or apparently insignificant. This is the type of experience we observe in Antonio, for example, in several scenes in which he allows himself to be transformed by opening his eyes to the beauty of the simple objects in his natural environment. Anaya has occasionally described this experience using a term invented by the poet Gerard Manley Hopkins, "inscape," by which is meant a type of mystical illumination or insight into the fundamental order and unity of all of creation.

CULTURAL CONTEXT

Family history and New Mexican history are inextricably linked in *Bless Me, Ultima*. Antonio's father, Gabriel Márez, teaches the young boy about his past, which is tied to the Spanish colonial period of the region. Gabriel is a *vaquero*, or cowboy, but this is more than just an occupation: it is a "calling" that has united Antonio's father and his paternal ancestors to the New Mexican plains, described as vast as the oceans. (Indeed, Antonio's father's surname, Márez, derives from the Spanish word *mar*, meaning the sea.) Social and economic changes in the state severely curtailed the free-spirited, aggressive lifestyle of the vaqueros, however, when Anglo settlers took control of the land. The novel refers to such background information as part of the process of Antonio's education concerning his family's past. These facts also serve to provide readers with the cultural and historical foundation that will broaden their appreciation of events in the novel.

Antonio's mother, María Luna, is also linked with local culture but from a different perspective, as her own surname, Luna, implies. (The Lunas are a people of the moon, tied to the land as farmers.) The Lunas represent a different tradition within the rural U.S. Hispanic culture of the Southwest: the farming tradition—settled, tranquil, modest, devout, tied to old ways and customs. María had convinced her husband to leave the village of Las Pasturas and a lifestyle she considered coarse and wild, to move the family to the town of Guadalupe, where better opportunities existed for their children. The move separates Gabriel from the other vaqueros and the free llano life he loves. He becomes a bitter man who drinks to soothe his hurt pride and his loneliness. The differences between these two cultures form the basis for the first major conflict affecting Antonio's family. These tensions, as we will discover in others throughout the work, are presented as dichotomies: Márez/Luna, vaquero/farmer, free-spirited/settled. Antonio must find a balance in these divided forces, which tug at him from opposite directions.

The first dream sequence in Chapter One illustrates his anxieties. Antonio describes a dream in which he witnesses his own birth assisted by an old midwife. After he is born she wraps up the umbilical cord and the placenta as an offering to the Virgin of Guadalupe, the patron saint of the town (and of Mexicans and Mexican Americans in general). In his dream Antonio observes a terrible quarrel between the two branches of his family. The Lunas hope that the baby will become one of them, or possibly even a priest (his mother's fervent hope); the Márez uncles smash the symbolic offerings of fruits and vegetables brought by the mother's clan, replacing them with their own emblematic gifts of a saddle, a bridle, and a guitar. They hope Antonio will follow their free-spirited ways.

Both families frantically attempt to take hold of the placenta, hoping to control the baby's destiny by disposing of it in their own allegorical fashion. The Lunas want to bury it in the fields, tying the boy to the earth; the Márez family wishes to burn it and scatter the ashes freely to the winds of the llano. The families nearly come to blows over the issue until the old midwife steps in, claiming her rights as the person who brought the young life into the world to dispose of the afterbirth herself.

That old midwife is Ultima, the *curandera*, or folk healer, who eventually comes to live in their home. One issue upon which both parents agree is their obligation to provide and care for the elders, respecting customs and traditions. Therefore, when Antonio's father discovers that Ultima will be living alone in the llano as people abandon the village of Las Pasturas, he and Antonio's mother decide to invite her into their household in gratitude for her years of service to them and the community. Ultima is a respected figure, referred to as "La Grande," the old wise one. Outside of the family, however, Ultima is feared by some. Her healing powers are suspect, and she is considered a *bruja*, or witch. The suggestion of witchcraft brings a shudder of fear to Antonio and is a warning to the reader as well; the idea that witches can heal but can also place and lift curses with evil powers is another example of Anaya's foreshadowing of things to come.

Ultima is associated with ancient traditions and wisdom; in *Bless Me, Ultima* she is also equated with the forces of nature. Her meeting with Antonio is accompanied by a whirlwind, an oft-repeated motif representing magical power and/or a warning of danger. As in traditional witch stories, Ultima is identified with a specific animal—in this case an owl. The animal is reputed to be a disguise assumed by witches, but Ultima's owl does not frighten Antonio. On the contrary, her owl protects, defends, and soothes him, an observation legitimized by another of Antonio's dreams in which the owl flies the Virgin of Guadalupe on its wings to heaven.

LANGUAGE

From the very first pages of the novel, Anaya interjects the Spanish language into the narration, in the form of individual words, characters' names, local references, and, on occasion, entire sentences of dialogue, as well as the chapter numeration. This interjection is accomplished with a naturalness that avoids interrupting the flow of the story. Spanish words are not italicized or differentiated in any way from the rest of the text, nor are there footnotes or a glossary to define them; rather, they are explained in a subtle, unobtrusive manner where appropriate. Occasionally an English equivalent will appear in sentences after a Spanish term has been introduced, or an explanatory phrase will clarify some term for those unfamiliar with the language. In several instances the syntax and phrasing of some of the dialogue in English sounds like a literal translation from Spanish. The bilingual use of language is limited but nonetheless effective in creating a distinctive tone in the novel. It is rationalized in the first chapter when Antonio affirms that the older people of his community speak exclusively in Spanish and that he himself learned English only after attending school (10). The use of Spanish is a carefully and minutely crafted device that is accepted by the reader as natural and logical, something not unexpected.

DREAM SYMBOLISM

Throughout *Bless Me, Ultima* Antonio's dreams serve several functions: they sometimes anticipate events to come, but more important they are an index to the main character's emotional and psychological development. Anaya has skillfully blended the external plot events with Antonio's frequent introspective musings and his world of dreams, a combination of personal experience, fantasy, and mythical legend. The blending is often achieved by the main character himself; reflecting on the importance of his dreams, Antonio will interpret their significance in the narratives that follow them. After the second dream in Chapter Two, which ends with his mother crying because Antonio is growing old (26), for example, the narrator begins the following chapter remarking on his fleeting youth (27), repeating the same message of his growing maturity. Indeed, Anaya leaves little to the reader's imagination regarding the interpretation of Antonio's dreams and other plot elements. The narrator often regulates our reading of the work by commenting on events and repeating their message. Comments such as "That is what Ultima meant by building strength from life" (247) ensure that the reader will remain on the right track.

Antonio's dreams pervade his waking hours; each influences to some degree his conduct and attitude. In Chapter Nine, for instance, aware that his brothers frequent "Rosie's house," the town brothel, Antonio's musings on his brothers' behavior mirror his own apprehensions with regard to women and sexuality, innocence and the concept of sin. The young boy represses his disturbing feelings by transferring them to a dream about his brothers' restlessness as they experience the restraints of a small town and their parents' aspirations. Their behavior is rationalized in the novel, in great part, by their lineage; the notion of blood and heredity is a motif throughout *Bless Me, Ultima*. Just as Gabriel's aggressiveness and María's gentle, subdued manner are understood as hereditary qualities in the "blood," Antonio's brothers' attitudes and actions are attributed to their father's character: "The Márez blood draws them away from home and parents" (72). Antonio's mother attempts to link his destiny with that of a Luna ancestor, a priest who supposedly established Guadalupe generations earlier. In his dream Antonio's brothers declare him to be a Luna who, for their mother's sake, will become a farmer-priest like their maternal ancestor. The dream sequences serve as good examples of the cross-weaving of the external and internal conflicts that drive the plot.

PLOT DEVELOPMENT

After her arrival in the home of Antonio's family, Ultima settles into a bucolic life. All the family members benefit from her presence: Antonio's mother is happy to share her days with another adult female, his sisters' chores are lessened with Ultima's assistance, and Antonio's father has someone to whom he can relate his frustrated dreams of moving westward to California with his older sons. World War II has taken them from his side, upsetting his plans. Antonio enjoys Ultima's presence as well; she is his mentor in the ways of nature and spirituality. This time of innocent joy gives way, however, to his first terrible experience of violence and death, to which Ultima's owl will sound a warning cry, as it does whenever it senses danger that could affect the family.

The dramatic events that propel the evolution of the main story (the external events that effect change in Antonio) are initiated dramatically in Chapter Two with the murder of the town sheriff, Chávez, and the revenge taken against his murderer, Lupito. Lupito is a disturbed man whose mind has been traumatized by war. His senseless killing of the sheriff incenses the men of the town, who form a search party to capture and punish the culprit. Hiding in bushes near the river, Antonio observes them. Despite attempts to sway the group, the men kill Lupito and thereby rouse Antonio's first doubts of conscience. Issues of right and wrong, guilt and innocence, the concept of God and justice are thoughts that assail his young, impressionable mind. This is the first of four tragic deaths that Antonio will encounter in a brief space of time. Ultima's influence is felt here too in the presence of her owl, which accompanies Antonio and calms his fears, temporarily dispelling his anxieties.

As in most novels of the coming-of-age genre, a significant element of the young narrator's development is his or her relationship with peers. School and a social network form a crucial component of the type of knowledge a young child will require to survive and flourish beyond the family orbit. Antonio is successful at making friends, among them Jason Chávez, Samuel, and Cico, who introduce him to a world of native legend and a type of spirituality and morality outside of official, established religion. The catechism lessons he studies in order to receive the sacrament of First Communion in the Catholic Church conflict with the folk traditions he learns from his friends. They propose an alternative religiosity and code of morality based on indigenous beliefs and offer a contrasting pagan deity to his family's devout Christianity. In Chapter Nine the boys relate the well-guarded secret of the golden carp (a secret known to few children and only to adults who, like Ultima, are "different"). The story is first told to Jason by the only Indian in town, a character referred to simply as "Jason's Indian." The legend holds that the carp had once been a god. The people who lived in that earlier time had sinned, and their punishment was to become fish. Loving his people, the god also became a fish to swim among them and protect them. The waters of the rivers and lakes that surround the town of Guadalupe hold other secrets as well, including that of a mermaid, a siren whose singing pulls those who hear it into the dark waters of the Hidden Lakes (115–117).

These stories create more religious dilemmas for Antonio, adding to his already confused spirituality. As in previous circumstances, Antonio confronts and partially resolves these conflicts in his dreams. In one dream the waters of the mermaid and the golden carp transform themselves into the stormy waters of his parents' fierce struggle over his future. The sweet water of the placid Luna moon tries to claim his loyalty, while his father rages that the salt water of the oceans is what truly binds him as a Márez. The conflict grows into a cosmic storm that threatens to destroy everything until Ultima intercedes. She brings peace to the dream (and to Antonio's tortured psyche) as she clarifies the meaning for Antonio, explaining that the moon and seas are not divided or distinct, but are, in fact, part of a holistic cycle of oneness, each replenished by the other.

Antonio's early doubts regarding established religion and conventional beliefs are heightened in Chapter Ten when the devoutly Catholic Lunas turn to Ultima to cure a family member who had been cursed by the three daughters of Tenorio Trementina, the town barber and owner of a run-down saloon. The women are believed to be witches and are referred to as "cohorts of the devil." María's brother Lucas had inadvertently witnessed one of their demonic rituals and had confronted them. Their evil powers bring him to death's door, and Ultima is summoned when Western medicine and the Catholic priest fail to break the spell. This chapter is one of the most effective in terms of creating an atmosphere of suspense and mystery. The narrator reiterates words that suggest wickedness and fear: sinister signs, Black Masses, the appearance of devils, and an "early horned moon" combine with familiar clichés regarding female witchcraft (for example, dancing with the devil, vulnerability to bullets etched with a sign of the cross, ritual sacrificing of animals, the use of dolls to create harmful spells). The drive to the Luna farm, normally a pleasant journey, is now "filled with strange portents," the atmosphere of the family home is "deathly quiet," and even the weather responds to psychic forces (90–91).

When Ultima confronts Tenorio and requests that his daughters cease their evil curse on Antonio's uncle or accept the consequences of their actions, a mournful whirlwind provides the background to the scene: the sky grows dark, blocking out the sun to produce an atmosphere described as "unnatural" (94–95). These and many other details contribute to the suspense that builds up to the process of the cure itself, a type of exorcism in which Ultima, with Antonio serving as his bewitched uncle's spiritual double, will rid Lucas of the evil curse. The three days that Antonio will suffer along with his uncle and his symbolic death and rebirth to save another are all part of Antonio's spiritual challenges. More powerful than the three witches and even more powerful than the priest and doctors, Ultima's faculties extend to retribution as well. Tenorio's daughters will pay for their crimes. One by one they fall ill and die. Ultima will be accused of witchcraft herself and put to the test by Tenorio and his friends, but her power is greater, and she is vindicated. Ultima's actions, however, set in motion the chain of events that will eventually lead to her own death at Tenorio's hands.

Chapter Fourteen combines many different plot elements that build toward the climax and contribute to the outcome of Antonio's ultimate understanding of himself. The chapter begins with Antonio's return to school, where he has found acceptance and a sense of belonging. It contains a rare note of humor in the depiction of the school Christmas play. A terrible blizzard prevents the girls of the school from attending and playing their assigned roles. The boys substitute grudgingly. The production is a calamity but ends in good-humored bedlam.

The relief of tension is short lived, however. Another of Tenorio's daughters falls ill, and he repeats his vow to kill Ultima and Narciso, a friend of the family. After school Antonio braves the blizzard alone and heads for home. He witnesses an argument between Tenorio and Narciso, who leaves to warn Ultima of the danger. Not realizing that he is being observed by Antonio, Narciso stops on his way at Rosie's brothel to warn Antonio's brother, Andrew, of Tenorio's plans. This scene adds to Antonio's confusion: Why does Narciso search for Andrew in such a place? Which Márez is Narciso calling for at the door? Could his own father be inside? In a prior dream Andrew had told Antonio that he would not enter Rosie's until his young brother had lost his innocence. Had young Antonio's experiences of death and violence, of magical cures and pagan gods, opened the path for sin to enter his soul? His crisis is exacerbated by his brother's appearance by the side of a young prostitute who convinces Andrew to remain with her instead of assisting Narciso. Still hidden by the storm, the boy observes Tenorio ambush Narciso and murder him.

Antonio runs home and informs his parents, succumbing to a fever and a terrible *pesadilla* (nightmare); his apocalyptic, end-of-the-world dream is one of the novel's most vivid. The main character's sense of confused guilt and terror fuses with figures and events from his past life in a chaotic frenzy. The thunderous voice of a vengeful God frightens the boy, who relives in his dream the murder, satanic rituals, and other forms of wickedness, as well as terrifying biblical tortures. The nightmare will end in resolution, however, effected by the healing power of nature. The golden carp swallows everything—good and evil—taking with it all the pain and strife of humanity. Antonio's subconscious discovers order and harmony in nature and native mythology.

Subsequent events in the novel continue to test the young boy's faith in God and humanity and the belief system he has been raised to maintain. In Chapters Seventeen and Eighteen the catechism lessons he must take fail to satisfy his spiritual needs. When a friend, Florence, challenges

Antonio's religious beliefs, schoolmates force Antonio to play the role of priest to punish Florence for his ideas. In several other instances Antonio inadvertently finds himself in that same role: "Bless me" are the final words he hears from Lupito before his violent death near the river, and Narciso's dying wish is for Antonio to hear his confession. The religious event that Antonio had so anticipated is disappointing; all the doubts he believed would be answered with the experience of First Communion receive no reply: "The God I so eagerly sought was not there, and the understanding I thought to gain was not there" (222).

Tenorio's threats against Ultima continue, but his evil extends to others as well. In Chapter Twenty a curse has been placed on a family that seeks Ultima's assistance. Stones rain from the sky on the Téllez family home, which even the priest's blessings were unable to prevent. Ultima determines that the curse was laid on a *bulto* (ghost) that haunts the house. The curse is linked in the novel with historical abuses against the indigenous peoples of the region. Ultima explains that the area was once the land of the Comanche Indians. Displaced by the Spaniards and Mexicans, three Indians had raided Téllez's grandfather's flocks for food and were hanged as punishment. As their bodies were not accorded a customary burial, their wandering souls can be used to harm others. Tenorio's daughters have awakened the Indian ghosts of the past to harm the Téllez family, but with Ultima's guidance a ceremonial cremation gives the Comanche spirits rest and eliminates the curse. Events such as these add to Antonio's anxieties and undermine his faith in God, who was not able to free the Téllez family from the curse.

The reappearance of the golden carp in the lake, however, soothes his worries: "Seeing him made questions and worries evaporate, and I remained transfixed, caught and caressed by the essential elements of sky and earth and water" (237). Antonio would like to share this feeling of tranquillity and illumination, "the beginning of adoration of something simple and pure" (238), with Florence, who had been alienated from Catholicism and spirituality by his own life experiences, but the protagonist will not get that opportunity. That same day Florence drowns in a tragic swimming accident in a forbidden section of the lake.

Antonio's family sends him to the Luna farm to rest from his terrible experiences and spend the summer assisting his uncles, a time he describes as "the last summer I was truly a child" (250). A heart-to-heart talk with his father during their trip to the farm brings them closer to an understanding, but trouble will reach Antonio even in this tranquil environment. Tenorio's second daughter has died, and he resolves again to take his vengeance. This time, however, he will attack Ultima's owl realizing that it is her very spirit.

After attempting to kill Antonio with his stallion, Tenorio makes for the boy's home. Antonio tries to warn Ultima, but he is too late. Tenorio points his rifle first at Antonio, but Ultima's owl takes the bullet in his place, mortally wounding her. "That shot destroyed the quiet, moonlit peace of the hill, and it shattered my childhood into a thousand fragments that long ago stopped falling and are now dusty relics gathered in distant memories" (258). Another attempt to destroy Antonio brings Tenorio's death, as he himself is killed by one of Antonio's uncles. The novel ends with Ultima's final blessing on the young boy, who gives her owl the burial Ultima has requested. The reader is left with the impression that Antonio will go on, better able to understand himself and find the answers he so wishes to discover.

CHARACTERIZATION

Bless Me, Ultima tells the story of an important relationship between a young boy and an old woman who helps him discover the beauty and complexity in life and in himself. As both protagonist and narrator, Antonio gradually reveals himself to the reader through his own words and through his dreams; he is both an evolving character and a narrating voice. Ultima, on the other hand, is revealed to us more by her actions and by the other characters' reactions to them. Many of the important events of the novel center on her. Her importance as a character is more functional: her character advances thematic concerns and helps to expose Antonio's qualities. Although less developed than Antonio's character, Ultima is integral to the novel nonetheless. As stated before, *Bless Me, Ultima* begins and ends with Ultima, and the relationship between her and Antonio propels the process of the boy-hero's development as a character.

Inquisitive and courageous, sensitive and thoughtful, Antonio's character evolves on several levels: on the objective, external plane his character passes through a variety of experiences, some typical of most young boys, some highly unusual. Many of his experiences can be compared to those of other rural Hispanic children in the U. S. Southwest of a certain era: he is raised in a Spanish-speaking home where traditions are maintained and respected; he confronts an Anglo-oriented school system where he is linguistically and culturally socialized into mainstream society; he is indoctrinated into the Catholic religion even as he is surrounded by competing influences.

Other experiences are less typical and even extraordinary: in a short period of time Antonio confronts violence and murder, tragic death, witchcraft, and supernatural phenomena. He will actively participate in ritual healing and even experience a symbolic death and rebirth as a part of his spiritual and psychological maturation. What Antonio cannot face or understand on a conscious level is deciphered in his dreams. His doubts and uncertainties are echoed on the subconscious level and occasionally resolved there as well. His reactions to these events as expressed in his dreams are the most revealing insights into the growth and evolution of the character, providing a thematic framework of his gradual transformation.

As noted earlier, Antonio's first dream is of his own birth; both his biological mother and his spiritual mother (Ultima) are present. The dreams that follow reflect concerns about family and fear of losses (of people and illusions) that prepare him for his passage into adulthood and individuality. The critic Vernon E. Lattin divides the nine remaining dreams that follow the birth sequence into groups that reveal the path to Antonio's destiny (" 'Horror of Darkness' " 51–57). Dreams three (45), five (70), and seven (140) reflect the fear of loss: Antonio foresees that he will not become the priest his mother had hoped for, his innocence will be lost as he faces the temptations of sexuality, and the vision of Ultima in her coffin foreshadows the loss through death of his spiritual mother. Dreams two (25), four (61), and nine (235) reflect anxieties concerning Antonio's brothers and the larger world beyond, foreshadowing the experience of loss that he must assimilate in order to attain adulthood. In dreams two and four Antonio's brothers confront their own destinies beyond the family. With Antonio's help they can face the dangers of the treacherous river, but Antonio comes to realize that he cannot always assist these giants of his dreams, and by dream nine he resigns himself to the fact that they are lost to him and to his parents. Like the souls of the Comanche spirits calmed by Ultima's ritual cremation, the souls of his brothers are put to rest in Antonio's anguished psyche.

Dreams six (119), eight (172), and ten (243) are considered by Lattin and other critics as the most significant, "the dreams most homologous with the experience of the sacred, and as they present the dark night of the soul, they prepare the soul for its rebirth" (Lattin, " 'Horror of Darkness' " 55). Dream six is the calm of reconciliation after the storm, an important step in solving Antonio's dilemma of good versus evil. The eighth dream becomes progressively more violent as despair and destruction are vividly communicated to the young boy: his home is set afire, his family is destroyed, Ultima is beheaded by an angry mob, and all life around him disintegrates. From this cosmic nothingness, regenerative powers emerge. Although Antonio's final dream, the tenth, is filled with the terror of death, the reader senses that he is now more prepared to accept and understand the realities of life. Having by now witnessed so much of Ultima's healing power, the messages of her teachings and of his own dreams have revealed themselves to him. Toward the novel's end he reflects: "And that is what Ultima tried to teach me, that the tragic consequences of life can be overcome by the magical strength that resides in the human heart" (249).

Ultima, as previously noted, is a less developed character than Antonio, but she is crucial nonetheless. At once a stabilizer and a catalyst for growth and change, the story revolves around the transference of her knowledge and worldview to Antonio. In Ultima Anaya has created a fascinating character who embodies the combination of indigenous traditions, ancient beliefs, and shamanic healing. Ultima is seer and natural scientist, teacher and herbal doctor. Despite her never having married or having had children of her own, she is a symbolic mother figure representing the mysteries of life, death, and transformation.

Ultima is a conciliatory force in the novel, guiding Antonio between the extremes of his parents and the myriad other tensions he must attempt to resolve. Respected as "una mujer que no ha pecado" (a woman who has not sinned) she is also feared. Her skills were acquired from a renowned healer, "the flying man of Las Pasturas," and hence many consider her a bruja. Ultima's characterization goes beyond the usual expectations regarding gendered roles for men and women because she is a curandera; she is afforded a place in the public world not usually given to women in traditional patriarchal cultures. Her power comes in part from her knowledge of herbal remedies, spiritual healing, and magical rituals. Her spiritual approach comes from numerous sources: from modern medicine, time-honored Native-American curative practices, Christianity, and pagan traditions. The complexity of this character derives from these differing sources that are blended in her. Ultima represents a Mexican/Amerindian tradition that has often been preserved precisely by women curanderas. Though uncommon in U.S. letters, curanderas have been a part of the Hispanic tradition for centuries and are familiar characters for many Hispanic readers.

Although somewhat ambiguous as to Ultima's status as a bruja, the novel clearly distinguishes between good and evil witches in its portrayal of Tenorio Trementina's three daughters. We learn of their practices through other characters. Tenorio himself is a troublemaker, his daughters bad-tempered and ugly. These characters are more stereotypical depictions of witches, participating in evil rituals with the devil, concocting terrible curses and brews, capable of assuming animal forms. Being labeled a bruja, however, is life threatening here, as evidenced in Tenorio's attempts to have Ultima declared a witch. A bruja is hated and feared even to the point of murder.

Tenorio and his daughters, along with other characters in the novel outside of Antonio and Ultima, are more functional than integral. They are one-dimensional and, in some cases, like that of the evil witches, little more than stereotypes. Some characters also serve an allegorical function, representing stages in Hispanic history in the region, recalling that the first Spanish settlers who arrived in the 1600s created a self-sufficient ranching and farming economy. In particular, the Márez side of Antonio's family epitomizes the early Spanish explorers, and the Lunas correspond to the brief Mexican period in New Mexico's history. (Critics believe that the reference to the Luna farmer-priest ancestor who settled the town is an allusion to the historical figure of Father José A. Martínez, a New Mexican clergyman in the nineteenth century who played a key role in the Taos revolt of 1846.)

THEMES

Given the density of symbolism, myth, and cultural references in *Bless Me, Ultima*, it is not surprising that the novel has inspired a variety of critical responses. On the most fundamental level the novel's major theme is the coming-of-age and self-realization of a young Hispanic boy in New Mexico. Other topics are the quest for personal and cultural identity, the significance of Chicano tradition and myth in spirituality and healing, and the role of mentors and guides in psychological and spiritual growth and development. Ultima fulfills that role in Antonio's life; her intimate knowledge of nature and healing introduces him to the sources that will facilitate his understanding of himself and his world. The varied elements in the novel that determine who the boy-hero will eventually become have prompted numerous and diverse readings of the novel.

Bless Me, Ultima emphasizes the protagonist's need to reconcile the opposites in his life. The novel offers numerous conflicts the young boy must confront and presents them as seemingly irreconcilable dichotomies. The most evident is the clash between his father's pastoral lifestyle and his mother's farming tradition. The differences between the two are repeated throughout the novel, underscored by their very surnames— Márez and Luna. Other striking examples are the conflicts between male and female, good and evil (personified in the beneficent mother figure Ultima versus the evil father Tenorio), love and hate, town and country, a Christian God versus the golden carp, and so forth.

Ultima's role is that of mediator, from the first dream in which she resolves the dispute between the two families who wish to control Antonio's destiny to the dream in which she reconciles the dichotomy of the waters of the sea and the moon by reminding Antonio that "the waters are one." Antonio, however, is also a mediator, searching for a middle ground, attempting to please both parents in the house they built in a space in-between them—not quite in the fertile valley but at the edges of the llano. The boy's chores will please both mother and father: he feeds the animals but also tries to create a garden from the rugged soil of the plains.

Some critics have also noted the message of reconciliation, synthesis, and harmony that is apparent in the novel. Conflicts and imbalances find a solution in harmony, balance, and a message of oneness; synthesis resolves opposites and mediates differences. Generally the balance and mediation is brought about by Ultima or Antonio; in other instances the wisdom of nature itself restores harmony.

Some readings of the novel portray it as a nostalgic text, romanticizing an era that has little relevance for contemporary Chicano readers, who are largely urban and for whom the conflicts among rural Hispanic traditions are issues of the past. Other critics disagree. For Horst Tonn, *Bless Me, Ultima* can be read on another level at which "the novel constitutes a significant response to relevant issues of the community. In broad terms, these issues are identity formation, mediation of conflict, and utilization of the past for the exigencies of the present" ("*Bless Me, Ultima*: Fictional Response" 2). At the time Anaya was writing his work the society of the United States was experiencing a crisis of values similar to that portrayed in the novel in the mid-1940s. The theme of the pressure of change portrayed in the novel that Tonn identifies is underscored in the scene in which the townspeople react to the detonation of the first atomic bomb near Alamogordo, New Mexico, in 1945: "They compete with God, they disturb the seasons, they seek to know more than God Himself. In the end, that knowledge they seek will destroy us all" (190).

The disruptive effects of World War II on veterans and their families, as well as the internal migration from rural areas to the cities, have their counterpart in the social upheavals of the 1960s, when Chicanos participated in movements for social change and began to question their cultural values and identities. *Bless Me, Ultima* proposes responses to the contemporary crisis of values based on the need for healing and reconciliation. Just as Antonio and Ultima function as mediators, healing a community suffering from strife and disruption, "the novel itself can be said to share in and contribute to a mediation process at work in the Chicano community during the 1960s and early 1970s" (Tonn, "*Bless Me, Ultima*: Fictional Response" 5). Juan Bruce-Novoa agrees that *Bless Me, Ultima* is truly a novel reflective of its era. In the midst of conflict and violence, some present at the time proposed the alternative responses of "love, harmony, and the brotherhood of all creatures in a totally integrated ecology of resources. . . . *Bless Me, Ultima* belongs to the counterculture of brotherhood based on respect for all creation" ("Learning to Read" 186).

ALTERNATIVE READING: ARCHETYPAL MYTH CRITICISM

An analysis of *Bless Me, Ultima* based on myth theory and criticism emphasizes the developing dream life of its protagonist and Anaya's expressed affinity for myth (see chapters 1 and 2 in this book). Myth theory and criticism examine such questions as the origin and nature of myth and the relationship between myth and literature. Scholars and critics who have attempted to respond to these issues have done so from such diverse disciplines as philosophy, psychology, anthropology, linguistics, folklore, and political science.

The ideas of psychiatrist Carl G. Jung have inspired many literary critics, particularly in the field of archetypal criticism. Although often used synonymously with myth criticism, archetypal criticism has a distinct history, evolving specifically from Jung's theory of archetypes. As was noted earlier in chapter 2, Jung was a student of Sigmund Freud, who referred to dreams as "the royal road to the unconscious." For Freud dreams reflected individual unconscious wishes and desires. Jung, on the other hand, believed that the recurrence of enduring symbols in dreams reflected a more universal and collective unconscious (inherited feelings, thoughts, and memories shared by all humans). He referred to the patterns of psychic energy that originate in the collective unconscious (and are normally manifested in dreams) as "archetypes" (the prime models upon which subsequent representations are based). The Jungian approach to mythology, therefore, is based on a belief of a common human access to the collective unconscious. Mankind in the modern world would encounter in dreams the same types of figures that appear in ancient and primitive mythology.

Jung described several of these archetypes specifically. Among them are the Shadow, the archetype of inherent evil; the Anima, the feminine principle that has multiple manifestations including the Earth Mother, the Good Mother, and its opposite, the Terrible Mother; and the Wise Old Man, who represents the enlightener, the master, the teacher. Often critics will use the term more loosely, referring to characters as archetypes to indicate that they represent universal principles. Rudolfo Anaya is well versed in these theories and has reflected on their validity: "One way I have in looking at my own work . . . is through a sense that I have about primal images, primal imageries. A sense that I have about the archetypal, about what we once must have known collectively" (Johnson and Apodaca, "Myth and the Writer" 422).

Bless Me, Ultima offers ample opportunities for archetypal interpretations. The archetypal feminine principle—the intuitive, loving, life-affirming protector and nurturer—can be attributed to Ultima, the Good Mother/Earth Mother, and on another level to the Virgin of Guadalupe, who appears often in Antonio's dreams and is his mother's spiritual protector. The Terrible Mother—the frightening female figure, emasculating and life threatening—corresponds to La Llorona, the legendary mother who destroyed her own children and threatens those of others. Female characters are presented as contrasts: Tenorio's daughters are the evil counterparts of Ultima's beneficent magic. The female temptress, representing female sexuality, appears on several levels: on the idealistic plane in the sirens and mermaids that lure men into dangerous waters but also in the prostitutes that work in Rosie's brothel, who cause men to stray from their rightful path. The archetypal Shadow is illustrated in numerous places, most obviously in the form of evil that Tenorio embodies, but the novel also teaches that evil can reside within people, hidden at a deeper level. Antonio's dreams, for example, force him to confront his own sinful temptations and self-doubts that must be overcome if he is to evolve and grow.

Antonio's character has been interpreted as that of the classic boy-hero who must successfully complete the universal rite of passage of separation, initiation, and return. He must depart the comforts of his mother's hearth and cross the bridge into the wide world of the town, with its perils and challenges. His trials will extend from witnessing Lupito's murder to actively participating in his uncle's ritual exorcism, during which he sacrifices himself for the sake of another. After three days of agony he will emerge as if reborn, a new, more mature boy who can reconcile himself with his father and mother and the world around him. Ultima provides him with the symbolic tools (her pouch of herbs) and the spiritual weapons (her teachings) that will assist him in this development.

A Jungian approach to *Bless Me, Ultima* could run the risk of leading to a static, unchanging mythical perception, however, one that certainly would not be faithful to Anaya's views on mythology. For the author mythology is not simply a refashioning or retelling of ancient or universal tales and patterns. Myths should speak to our contemporary lives, give significance to a community. Historically constructed over generations, myths can help us understand contemporary realities and conditions. A more dynamic approach to myth criticism in *Bless Me, Ultima* is described by Enrique Lamadrid as "an ongoing process of interpreting and mediating the contradictions in the everyday historical experience of the people" ("Myth as Cognitive Process" 103). In the novel this is manifested in the oppositions (for example, good versus evil, love versus hate) that are mediated by Ultima and Antonio. Their role is to reconcile these contradictions to arrive at harmony and synthesis and, in keeping with the original role of myth, resolve the internal schisms of their community.

A myth criticism interpretation of *Bless Me, Ultima* should bear in mind, however, that Anaya describes a specific culture, a particular belief system. An analysis of the character of Ultima may reflect universal principles, but it must be remembered that Ultima, as a shaman/curandera, represents an actual vocation, that of a healer or spiritual leader, a role with a useful and important function in an authentic culture. The role of the shaman and that of the curandera are often indistinguishable. Both can resort to dreams and visions for help and guidance; both practice medical, magical, and spiritual arts. A specialist in the use of spells and incantations as well as herbal remedies, the shaman is believed to have the power to change her or his human form into that of an animal or spirit (see discussion of shamanism in chapter 8 herein). The curative practices of a curandera are intertwined with religious beliefs and respect for nature. Disharmony and imbalance cause a disruption of health; healing is a return to oneness and harmony with nature.

These alternative healing values have endured for centuries and continue to provide contemporary answers to age-old questions. *Bless Me, Ultima* demonstrates that myth criticism and a culturally specific approach to a work of literature need not be mutually exclusive. Anaya's novel is historically relevant and magical, both ancient and contemporary.

4

Heart of Aztlán
(1976)

After the success of *Bless Me, Ultima*, the first-person recollection of a young Hispanic boy in the rural New Mexico of the mid-1940s, Rudolfo Anaya's second novel addresses the displacement of this same group of people from the *llanos* (plains) of New Mexico to the urban *barrios* (neighborhoods) of Albuquerque. The second novel of his New Mexico trilogy (see chapter 2 in this book), *Heart of Aztlán*, further develops a favored Anaya theme that connects the spiritual well-being of the Chicano community with its ties to the land and to myth—in this case the myth of the legendary Aztlán.

Critical response to *Heart of Aztlán* was less favorable than that to Anaya's first novel. The attempt to blend a sociopolitical theme with mystical elements was perceived as contrived and simplistic. Critics viewed the work as disjointed, unconvincing in its characterizations, less polished than *Bless Me, Ultima*, and lacking the depth and meticulous prose style of Anaya's earlier work. The novel's redeeming qualities were not overlooked, however: "its treatment of the urban experience and the problems inherent therein, as well as . . . its attempt to define the mythic dimension of the Chicano experience" (Lewis, "Review" 74). The novel is fittingly dedicated to the people of the barrio of Barelas, Anaya's own neighborhood as a young teenager in Albuquerque, and to all those who struggle for justice and dignity.

POINT OF VIEW AND LANGUAGE

Heart of Aztlán is narrated in the third person, a departure from Anaya's use of the first person in his previous novel. Unlike first-person
narration, which is limited to the perspective of a central character, a
third-person omniscient (all-knowing) narrator has unrestricted knowledge of events, thus broadening the scope of a work. Written in English,
this novel is interspersed with words and phrases in standard Spanish
and the language of the "pachucos,"* thereby characterizing the social
and linguistic realities of the barrio culture depicted in the work. As in
Bless Me, Ultima, Anaya's linguistic patterns take shape from the very
beginning of the novel, which explains that the characters speak either
in the Spanish language of their home and community or in the English
of their educational environment: "they moved in and out of the reality
which was the essence of each language" (2).

While most of the novel is narrated in standard English, scholar Roberto Cantú notes that on occasion the narrator undermines the distance
usually afforded by third-person narration by adopting a pachuco "discourse" ("The Surname" 299). In the first chapter the words spoken by
the pachucos are described as a "strange, mysterious argot" (10), unfamiliar to the rural Chávez family. With time, however, pachuco vocabu-
lary begins to permeate the narrative. Cantú gives the example of one
scene in which the young men from the barrio, the *vatos locos* (literally
"crazy guys" or "crazy dudes"), get high on *mota* (marijuana) (41). The
narrator gradually employs pachuco language as if from within—that is,
as if identified with the characters themselves—without recourse to
translation or explanation for the reader.

Although Spanish and pachuco words are not translated, this not does
significantly hinder the reader's appreciation. On the contrary, it provides an authentic tone and flavor to the work and conveys a sense of
community. Anaya is sensitive to the oral tradition and the everyday
spoken idiom (it should be noted that Anaya does privilege Spanish-
speaking readers with an "insider's" appreciation of certain words, usually in the form of profanities and common expressions). The author's

*"Pachuco" is a term that was originally applied in the 1940s to zoot-suited Chicano youths
in large urban areas. It has become a more generalized term to describe Chicano "dudes"
from the barrio, with their characteristic form of language, dress, and behavior.

use of Spanish stems from his desire for authenticity and his bilingual and multicultural experiences.

In some cases the inclusion of Spanish words conveys an even more profound significance. In the first chapter, for instance, the land that the Chávez family must leave behind is described as "sacred," repeated in Spanish and italicized: *"La sagrada tierra"* (4). The multiplicity of connotations of *tierra* in the Spanish language—property, the soil, the nation or motherland, and the planet—are far-ranging and reveal the complex and intimate relation of Hispanic cultures to the land (similar to that of other traditional peoples). For some, the fact that Anaya has written his novels in English to transmit these ideas means more than simply adding another contribution to the body of American letters: the author "validates [English] as a transmitter of Chicano lore. Anaya is, quite simply, giving the old myths a new home" (Taylor, "The Mythic Matrix" 203).

PLOT DEVELOPMENT

In the first chapter of *Heart of Aztlán* the reader confronts a group of people in transition. The Chávez family—Clemente; his wife, Adelita; and four of their five children, Jason, Benjie, Juanita, and Ana—are leaving the small town of Guadalupe, New Mexico, for Albuquerque. Away from the deserted pueblos and llanos, past the mountains, they are headed for "a new time in a new place" (2). The reaction of each member to the move varies. The work opens with young Benjie's perspective, an excited anticipation of adventure in the big city, away from the small-town monotony of Guadalupe. His older brother Jason is more thoughtful, aware of the disturbances the move will produce in his father, Clemente, who was forced to sell the land settled by his ancestors in order to pay his debts. The move produces a pain in Clemente compared to having "the roots of his soul pulled away" (3).

The first chapter situates the Chávez family within a wider sociohistorical context. The Chávezes and their neighbors are part of a widespread internal migration from the rural areas of New Mexico to the urban centers of the state and as far away as California. All vow to return home one day but are rarely able to do so. Clemente recalls the process of losing the land as an event that began much earlier with the arrival of the *tejano* (Texans) and the new laws imposed by the Anglo settlers. From their origins on the plains, then on to a small town, and now to the city, the Chávez family searches for a better life with more opportunities for their children. They will carry with them their memories of the past and a coffee tin that Adelita fills with earth to remain in touch with their origins.

The family's destination is the Chicano barrio of Barelas, a crowded, dusty section of Albuquerque. Their married older son, Roberto, already lives in Barelas and has prepared for their arrival. In Barelas they encounter old friends and neighbors from home and make new acquaintances, among them Crispín, an old blind poet/seer whose blue guitar plays "magical" music (14). References to magic of a different sort emerge as well. A neighbor warns of an old witchlike woman with a *piedra mala* (evil stone) that can make predictions and "sing" the secrets of the heart.

Allusions are also made to a character from Anaya's first novel, in which Jason was a minor character. In *Bless Me, Ultima,* Jason had an Indian friend who revealed mystical secrets to him, including that of the magical golden carp of the river (see chapter 3). Jason's old Indian friend, who had related the power of magic stones to him back in Guadalupe, is mentioned in *Heart of Aztlán* as having been a friend of Crispín. His prior mystical experiences in Guadalupe will follow Jason to Barelas, where they will continue in his relationship with Crispín; the magic stone will play an important role in his family's life later in the story.

The family's first day in Albuquerque ends on an ominous note. The youngest son, Benjie, has already been introduced to gang life and drug use; and a police siren, recalling the wailing sound of the legendary La Llorona, the fearful destroyer of children, cries through the barrio as it searches for young lawbreakers, mixing with the roaring sound of the railroad yard, a constant rumbling of trains that "thrashed about like snakes in a pit" demanding service (18). Clemente will be among the workers who provide that service in a workplace described as a hellish labyrinth; the black steel water tank inscribed with the railroad name of Santa Fe (Holy Faith) looms over the barrio, surrounded by serpentine trains that writhe around and, when coupled, give "unnatural birth to chains of steel" among thunderous blasts of steam, spewing soot on the workers, houses, and trees nearby (22). Jason hears a worker refer to it as the "devil's place" when he delivers his father's lunch to him at work.

On Clemente's first day on the job Jason witnesses a terrible accident that claims a worker's life in a scene compared to an ancient blood sacrifice to the gods (23). Responsibility for the frequent workplace accidents is placed on uncaring, exploitative bosses and on a corrupt union that defends the company's interests over those of the workers. Unable to accept such sudden and violent death, Jason searches for Crispín, recalling an Indian belief in the power of song to "touch the stream of life and death" (26). Crispín helps the young man face his shocked grief and narrates the origins of his blue guitar, accompanied in the novel with an italicized mythic version of the same tale. The origins of the land of Aztlán are combined with Crispín's mission to sing the songs of past and future, joining his songs with those of others.

Clemente's authority as head of the family begins to erode as a result of the move to the city and as his children gain greater independence from their father. His two daughters defy him openly, demanding a freedom that they believe should accompany their new economic self-sufficiency, and Benjie becomes increasingly more involved with illegal drug and gang activities. Adelita has adapted more easily to the changes of city life, seemingly more flexible and unafraid than her husband; Clemente begins to resent her and drinks to soothe his hurt pride. The stresses sharpen during a wedding party at which Jason confronts two gang members, Frankie and Flaco, who threaten Benjie. Although Jason's status in the neighborhood increases due to his valorous defense of his brother, Clemente reacts violently to Benjie's gang activities, beating his son as never before in an attempt to recapture his eroded parental authority. Even as he does so, however, he realizes his error: "a cleavage had come between father and son. He cursed the city and blamed himself for even having come to it" (43).

Jason has now formed his own group of friends, a gang of young men that includes "crazy Willie," who, despite his nickname and his strange family background, is among the more thoughtful members of the group. Their conversations revolve mostly around girls, usually from a sexist perspective, and their summer experiences will include a visit to the local brothel, the "Golondrinas," and a party at Cindy Johnson's, a gabachita, or rich white girl, from the "County Club district" of the city who is infatuated with Jason. Whereas in Chapter Three a Hispanic wedding celebration is described with the traditional music and customs, in Chapter Five Cindy's party reflects a parallel Anglo culture that exists outside the barrio in Anglo society. Cindy teaches Jason bebop dance steps to the music of Bill Haley and Little Richard as she represents her world of privilege and wealth. Despite Cindy's tempting advances, Jason is attracted to Cristina Sánchez, the daughter of the man whose death he had witnessed in the railroad yard. She has attended Cindy's party with Sapo, a violent young man who leads a rival gang and has vowed to confront Jason. A later meeting with Jason will only frustrate Sapo's plans, however. Jason deftly manages to escape harm to himself and his friends by kicking a gun out of Sapo's hand and fleeing from his enraged aggressor.

On the same day, Jason visits Willie's home and his eccentric family, a reclusive group that includes Rufus, his junk-collecting father, and an abnormal brother, Henry, who remains separated from the rest of the family and chained to a tree to avoid being institutionalized. Feared and shunned by their neighbors, Willie's family members have retreated into themselves, causing Jason to reflect on his own father's loneliness, separated from his roots and his people.

Clemente's family problems continue throughout the fall as his younger daughter, Ana, decides to drop out of high school. Both daughters feel trapped in a hopeless situation in which the only way out appears to be dead-end jobs. Ana is attracted to the pachuco lifestyle and identifies with their open, defiant view of the world, even tattooing a blue ink dot on her forehead. However, her older sister, Juanita, disagrees that the pachucos are completely free from rules, observing that their sexist attitudes toward women are simply an alternative version of oppressive ideas (70).

The person least able to adapt to Barelas is Clemente. His increased drinking has estranged him further from his family, and he now unjustly blames his wife for usurping his dominant place in the home, permitting the children to become more independent. Frustrated in his family life, Clemente has also lost his economic security since he and some other workers have been precluded from working in the railroad yards by the corrupt union leader, Kirk. The men had attended an unauthorized workers' meeting to elect their own union president and have therefore been blacklisted; jobs are closed to them throughout the city. Through all their problems Adelita remains loyal to her husband, recalling their youth in Guadalupe, where her husband proudly walked his lands. Separated from his circle of support, she describes him as "a man lost in a foreign land" (78).

Clemente's and his coworkers' employment problems are worsened by the corrupt union representation of Kirk, who has illegally ratified a new contract after fixing the workers' votes. Lalo, a radical dissident union leader, organizes an unsuccessful wildcat, or unofficial, strike. The striking workers are quickly replaced by other men desperate for any work, regardless of the poor wages and conditions. Unemployed and dejected, the former workers strive desperately for solutions. All agree that a legitimate leader must be found to organize their efforts for justice, but Lalo is not to their liking. He preaches armed revolution for a radical change in the social system, but he lacks the workers' trust. The meeting ends with Crispín's songs, the *corridos* (ballads) of past revolutions and ancient heroes. His songs remind them of the "mythical land of Aztlán" (83), the legendary place of their Aztec origins in the U.S. Southwest, and of the need for a renewed leadership. Fascinated by Crispín's story, Clemente still cannot make a connection between the myth and his own reality. Some of the men had looked in his direction at the mention of a new leader, but Clemente is not prepared for the position yet; he must first search for something to relieve his personal inner anxieties.

His thoughts turn to the old woman and the strange power of the evil stone as a possible solution. Clemente searches for her in the darkness, wandering in circles near the river. Frightened and lost, he comes upon the bizarre figure of a naked man dancing and praying to the moon (Willie's brother, Henry). He finally meets up with the old woman and enters her house, a foul ominous hut filled with herbs and rotted animals. The "ancient and divining stone" (88) beckons, but Clemente is not prepared to meet its conditions: he must sell his soul for its power. An attempt to grab the rock gives him a shock and burns his hands. Clemente has not yet reached the point where he can accept the power of the stone.

In Chapter Nine two rival youth factions, the Hispanic pachucos and the young Anglo cowboys, will fight each other at the state fair. Even their girlfriends join in. Winter is fast approaching, and Rita, Clemente's daughter-in-law, has given birth to a baby boy. The traditional baptism is held in the church, but the fiesta that follows is given equal importance as it represents the baby's entrance into the love of the community (100). Admiring glances toward the baby are considered a threat; they can cast the "evil eye," a long-held superstition. The men discuss the boy's future, believing he will follow in his father's footsteps in the railroad yard.

Roberto wants more for his son, however. He dreams of a formal education for the baby, trusting that in that manner he will return one day to the barrio to improve conditions there. Others disagree. They have seen those who have become alienated from their people by an education and fear it can destroy their way of life. Clemente proposes that perhaps his grandson will become the leader for whom they are searching. Crispín is asked if indeed the Chávez baby is the one who will lead his people. Touching Clemente's shoulder, Crispín whispers an ambiguous reply: "It is true, this Chávez will lead" (102). Clemente is shaken by the possible meaning of the old man's words—which Chávez is he referring to?—while the men continue to reflect on the past: the loss of the old traditions and their communal lands, their dispersal to the slums of the city. In the evening, after all have left, the baby falls ill. His sickness is in fact caused by the evil eye, cast inadvertently by the character Dorotea, who insists on curing the child herself in the traditional manner. She does so, using "the remedies of faith" (105).

Chapter Eleven opens with a reflection on life, death, and "deer moons" in late autumn. Jason and his friend Chelo remark on the size of the enormous autumnal moon when they suddenly notice that Henry has freed himself from his chains and is headed for the irrigation canal, leaping for joy at the moon. Henry is reaching out dangerously at the moon's reflection in the water when the current drags him under. Chelo prevents Jason from attempting to save Henry, knowing that Henry's strength would cause them both to drown.

Henry's drowning is followed in Chapter Twelve by an introductory italicized mythic passage in which his death is compared to a mystical sacrifice: *"South of Aztlán the golden deer drank his fill and tasted the sweet fragrance of the drowned man's blood. That evening he bedded down with the turtle's sisters and streaked their virgin robes with virgin blood"* (112). Henry's body is discovered by a fisherman in the river. The coroner tries to prevent Rufus from claiming his son's sparse remains, and the priest refuses to grant him a traditional *velorio* (wake), but Rufus stubbornly carries the heavy casket home on his back. News of the tragedy spreads, and slowly Rufus's neighbors, who had formerly shunned him, follow him in a sad procession through the streets of the barrio. They help prepare the house for the traditional gathering with gifts of food and drink, and the old man Lazaro arrives to recite the prayers. According to the narrator, the velorio celebrates life's brevity and reaffirms shared humanity (118).

With half of the men out of work, the winter season is harsh in the Barelas barrio. Some neighbors return to their villages, but most remain in the city, where those who still have jobs suffer in the dangerous railroad shops. Clemente's drinking and despair have led him to hit bottom; he trips and falls into a gutter, where he welcomes the thought of death. Called to Clemente's side by an inner voice, Crispín struggles to carry Clemente to safety. He urges Clemente to seek his life's purpose in the "heart of Aztlán" (122). He tells Clemente the legendary story of Aztlán and speaks of the magical "singing rocks" and their secrets. Clemente's journey will take him back to the old woman and the piedra mala. With the help of the stone's magic and with Crispín's guidance, Clemente voyages to a land of ancient gods, sacred lakes, deserts, and mountains, to a river of suffering people, and finally to the "dark womb-heart of the earth," where he is empowered by his vision to cry out, "I AM AZTLÁN!" (131), feeling himself one with the masses that surround him, transformed by his mystical experience.

When Clemente returns to the barrio, ill and speaking of having been "touched by the heart of the earth," people believe him to be mad. His wife and children are also at pains to understand him. Clemente resolves to find a leader to help his people and seeks the advice of the Catholic priest, Father Cayo. Although the priest had not supported the workers in the past, Clemente hopes to convince him to attend the workers' meeting and help end the injustices. Father Cayo consents to meet with Clemente, but he does not respond in the manner Clemente had anticipated. The priest first admonishes Clemente fiercely for having sought the old woman's magical powers and then adamantly refuses to speak out against the abuses of the railroad bosses. The Church must care for souls, he explains, and not engage in political struggles. It is a part of the status quo, the social hierarchy that is comprised by "the government, the banks, the military," and each of these elements must support the others to remain in power (143).

At the workers' meeting Lalo encourages the men to fight abuse with armed struggle, but they are wary of the dangerous consequences. Clemente calls for unity based on their mutual bonds, "el alma de la raza," the soul of the people. Unsure of his own words, Clemente calls for a "rekindling" of their spirits, but his message is misconstrued. The men take to the streets with torches against the railroad; they set fire to an old shack. The police respond, killing several of the men. Clemente's next move is to approach a successful Chicano grocery store owner, Mannie Garcia, referred to as "el Super," in hopes that he can be persuaded to lead the people. El Super is not interested, however; he disdains his own people, and no money can be made in what Clemente offers. Envy, he claims, will eventually destroy any leader who rises to the top, and he wants no part of it.

In Chapter Sixteen Jason and his young friends get together and analyze, in their own words, the situation in the barrio from their perspective. The same message of the lack of support by the Church and the business community, as well as the need for Chicano unity reflected in the previous chapter, is repeated in the discussions of the younger characters, with an additional antiwar sentiment expressed by Jessie Martínez, a Korean War veteran they encounter in Conio's café. Suffering from post-traumatic symptoms, Jessie had been considered a war hero upon his return to Barelas, but he was demoralized by his war experience. Jason's friends begin to think of their own futures of marriage and settling down. The reader also learns that a rumor has spread in the barrio that Cindy is pregnant and Jason is the father, a rumor he denies. Jealous of Jason's relationship with Cristina, Cindy has vengefully invented the story.

In the following chapter Willie informs the gang of an attempt by the business community, with el Super and Father Cayo as its spokespeople, to bribe Clemente. Fearing his growing influence in uniting the people, they offer Clemente money and threaten to have him arrested if he will not accept their terms. Clemente angrily refuses, magically setting their money to flames with his touch. As a result of this encounter, Clemente's influence among the people grows even greater.

It is the Christmas season, and Jason and his friends head for the church where the girls are assisting in the decorations. Jason goes there to be with Cristina, but el Super's wife, a meddling gossip referred to as "la Lengua" (the tongue), spreads the word that Jason is the father of Cindy's child. Cristina's mother and the priest unfairly denounce Jason, who is forbidden to see the girl. Cristina later runs into Sapo, who reveals the truth regarding Cindy's baby: Benjie, Jason's brother, is actually the father. Jason sees Cristina and Sapo at a dance, and a fight breaks out. Sapo grabs Cristina and takes off, first shooting Frankie, who is saved from death by Crispín's magical music, and then vowing to kill Benjie, who he forces at gunpoint to climb the steel water tank at the railroad yard. Jason attempts to stop Sapo from shooting his brother, but Sapo fires nonetheless, shattering Benjie's left hand before he falls to the ground. Benjie is left alive but paralyzed.

The final chapter opens with an italicized passage in which a golden deer stands still and then leaps to the north toward his people; the passage is followed by a parallel paragraph of narrative describing a deer in the pink forests seeking protection while the new moon smiles in a colorless, threatening sky. The people of the barrio are now aware of the tragic events that have affected Clemente's family, and one of them, Manuel, relates Clemente's reaction to his son's misfortune. Clemente has vented his rage on the railroad water tank, slamming it repeatedly with a sledgehammer and his fists, going into shock as a result.

Slowly his story spreads throughout the barrio, and the people begin to gather in support at his home. Strengthened by their solidarity, Clemente calls Crispín to his side and asks him to play a drumming sound on his guitar as he addresses the people. Clemente raises a torch and speaks of the true fire that will defeat their exploiters, "the fire of love that burns in each man and woman and child; it is the fire of the soul of our people which must serve us now!" (208). The novel concludes with Clemente leading an emboldened procession singing revolutionary songs and fearlessly shouting, "¡Adelante!" (Forward!) (208–209).

NARRATIVE STRATEGIES

As in *Bless Me, Ultima*, Anaya utilizes italics to distinguish the differing levels of time and space in the narrative. Whereas italics were used in his first novel primarily to describe the protagonist's dreams, the numerous italicized segments of *Heart of Aztlán*, which vary in tone and rhythm from the rest of the narration, link the story to an alternative, spiritual reality. The ongoing actions of the plot are thus tied to an enduring, mythical past. When Adelita fills a coffee can with earth from her old home to remind the family of the land they are leaving, for example, the italicized passage that follows underscores an ageless indigenous myth: centuries earlier, we are told, an Indian woman performed the same ritual as the people "*wandered across the new land to complete their destiny*" (7). These passages provide a mythical-symbolic dimension that amplifies and enriches the focus and emotional impact of the novel.

As the second novel of a trilogy, the expected references to an earlier work are present in *Heart of Aztlán*. Antonio Márez from *Bless Me, Ultima*, referred to as Anthony in *Heart of Aztlán*, is mentioned as Jason's young friend; and "the old woman who could fly" is a reference to Ultima (14). The town of Guadalupe and Jason's Indian friend are among the additional setting and character references that link the two books.

Mythical motifs (reiterated themes or patterns) in *Bless Me, Ultima* are also repeated in *Heart of Aztlán*, most notably, the legendary wailing woman figure of La Llorona, who evolves from a terrifying female force of destruction in *Bless Me, Ultima* to a more contemporary destroyer of Chicano males. In *Heart of Aztlán*, La Llorona takes the form of the piercing whistle of the railroad yards and the sound of police sirens. But *Heart of Aztlán* includes literary references from beyond the Anaya repertoire as well. An admirer of the poet Wallace Stevens, Rudolfo Anaya fashioned the character of Crispín from Stevens's "The Man with the Blue Guitar," itself an allusion to a painting by Pablo Picasso. The name Crispín is also that of a Stevens character from another of his poems, "The Comedian as the Letter C."

Heart of Aztlán presents part of the first year of a family's new life in a new city. The novel begins with the family's move from a rural home to an urban barrio in the summer season. Their problems increase in the "dying" season of autumn, only to culminate during the stresses of winter (Clemente's personal crisis, Jason's romantic relationship, the workers' joblessness), a season of darkness when the illumination of the sun is at its weakest. Clemente's spiritual journey to a mountain in the north corresponds to the Native-American myth of man's beginnings; the seasonal division of the novel—which has among its themes the lack of spiritual leadership in the Chicano community—suggests the Hopi ceremonial year, which is void of spiritual beings (leaders) from August to January (Gerdes, "Cultural Values in Three Novels of New Mexico" 244).

THEMES

Heart of Aztlán is a story of the changes that the displacement from a rural to an urban life have brought about in the life of a Chicano family. An explicitly political novel, the work nevertheless shares on another level the mythological themes that characterize most of Rudolfo Anaya's writing (see chapter 2 herein). It reconciles a people's legends and myths with their daily lives. Some critics consider the novel's blending of legend and myth with social critique an important contribution to the tradition of Chicano novels; negative criticism of the work stems precisely from the challenges of combining these two approaches in a plausible manner. Some have found the novel to be simplistic and didactic, lacking the harmonious cohesion of *Bless Me, Ultima*, in which there is more organic unity between myth and reality, mystical message and plot development. Among the novel's messages or themes are the following.

Displacement and Disintegration

The need to adapt to a hostile urban environment effects a change on each individual member of the Chávez family in various and diverse ways (see the "Characterization" section below), but, in general, the move to Barelas has consequences that are profoundly experienced by all: the need to forge new urban identities, the fragmentation and disruption of family life, moral disintegration, the loss of paternal authority, the negative influence and brutality of drugs and gang culture, the lack of employment and educational opportunities, social neglect, abuse and discrimination, the erosion of traditional values. Their original reasons for moving were based on larger economic factors beyond their control, and the problems they must face as a result are not entirely of their own making. Although presented from the point of view of an individual family, the novel is clearly understood to reflect a larger historical, collective process affecting an entire ethnic group in a particular place and time.

Social Exploitation

From the first chapter of the novel it is clear that a central focus of the work is the struggle for workers' rights. The Chávez family will confront the death and abuse of workers from the very beginning, and, indeed, Clemente's struggle will be to find a means to inspire his neighbors to liberate themselves from these conditions. The barrio of Barelas is impotent, however, paralyzed by the oppression of its employers and the corrupt unions that misrepresent the people. The towering steel water tank that overlooks the railroad yard ironically proclaims a new "Holy Faith," the technology of modern U.S. society that looms ominously over the barrio reminding its inhabitants of their lack of power and control. Other culprits are Mannie, "el Super," who has learned how to benefit from the capitalist system while he egotistically ignores the plight of his own Chicano people, and Father Cayo, who dismisses the everyday needs and suffering of his parishioners, claiming that his role as a priest is purely spiritual as he sides with their abusers.

The mainstream society of the United States does not escape criticism, however; Barelas has been the victim of its neglect as well. The problems of Chicanos and Hispanic peoples are not limited to a single barrio. The novel's criticism of social discrimination and the lack of educational and employment opportunities, as well as the condemnation of the traumatic effects of war on young poor men who have fought for liberties abroad that they do not enjoy at home, among other issues, crosses geographic boundaries.

The solutions to some of the issues described above are implicit: more educational opportunities for Chicanos, better worker representation, a church more attuned to social injustice, and so forth. Yet these sociopolitical problems require changes that, according to the novel, are not simply political or ideological. Change also requires spiritual growth on a personal and a communal level for social struggles to succeed. One example is the problem of corrupt union representation. The more radical, violent proposals represented by Lalo are rejected as futile responses to the technological power and control of the capitalist oppressors. *Heart of Aztlán* proposes another solution, in keeping with Anaya's vision of the power of myth and culture. To better understand Anaya's mythical message, one must first become familiar with the myth of Aztlán from which the title of the work and its ideas are derived.

The Myth of Aztlán

As noted in chapter 2 of this book, the era of the 1960s was one of heightened analysis and self-awareness within U.S. ethnic and racial minority groups. As the Chicano people demanded social justice for their communities, they also demanded their rights to reclaim lost cultural identities and affirm the validity of their roots in U.S. society. In many cases this task meant the articulation of values that were in contrast and opposition to Anglo culture. Part of the articulation of countervalues extended to the construction of countermyths, such as the promotion of the mythological Aztlán, the ancestral home of the Aztecs, or *mexicas*, in the U.S. Southwest (a geographic area approximately stretching from present-day Texas, Colorado, Utah, and California to the Rio Grande). Aztlán was considered not only a territorial challenge but also a symbol of Chicano cultural origins, unity, and self-determination. The presence of the Chicano ancestors in the area preceding that of the Anglo Americans gave the former a moral right to these lands.

Significantly for our understanding of *Heart of Aztlán*, the legend revives Native-American myths and symbols rooted in Aztec lore, considered a part of the collective Chicano history. According to this legend, seven tribes left their seven mountain caves in Aztlán because they were told in prophesy to migrate south, where they would discover a place in which they could establish a new civilization. That place was Tenochtitlán (present-day Mexico City), a spot they would recognize by a sign: an eagle perched on a nopal cactus with a snake in its claws.

Anaya interprets the legend as a hopeful lesson for his community, a lesson that involves tapping further into human potential, creating a world without limitations and man-made borders. "This is the legacy of

Aztlán: it is a place where seven tribes of humankind came to a new awareness of their potential, a new sensitivity in their relationship to earth and cosmos. [They] took their destiny into their own hands, they were born into a new prophesy, and they moved to complete it. Can we do less?" ("Aztlán" 383).

Ancient Legends and Modern Solutions

How does a legend like the myth of Aztlán apply to contemporary issues? While such ideas have been utilized as a unifying device in political struggles, for Anaya myths can also serve a more profound, spiritual purpose: the healing of a community and a culture. Thus, though events in the novel may originate in ancient legends, Anaya adapts these to present-day circumstances: an italicized segment about ancient sacrificial rites follows the death of a Chicano worker in the railroad yard (25); the eagle and serpent of the Aztec culture are reinterpreted in Crispín's call for a leader who will rise like an eagle to conquer the "steel snakes" of the railroad (184). From where will such power emerge? From the heart of Aztlán, not an actual place (Clemente's magical pilgrimage will teach him that lesson), but the healing power of discovering the purpose of one's life, in spiritual union with one's people, whose social paralysis and collective suffering must be cured if their culture is to survive.

It should be noted that Anaya has not confined himself to Aztec myths in this novel for his reinterpretation of ancient legends. The Llorona legend of the Hispanic tradition is repeatedly found in one form or another in many of his works. In *Heart of Aztlán* her frightful cries, as noted earlier, become the piercing whistles at the railroad shops and the sirens of police cars. The golden deer mentioned frequently in its race across the sky combines the solar symbolism of Aztec myths with the totemic animal of Native-American Pueblo culture.

The shamanic motifs found in most Anaya novels are present here as well. Clemente's symbolic ascent to the mountain is arrived at through an encounter with a powerful object (the evil stone) in the hut of an old witch. Crispín is the shaman and guide who will assist Clemente in linking reality with myth, the problems of the barrio with the vision of Aztlán. Clemente's classical mythological journey or quest is not necessarily to the past, however, but to his own heart, where he will find his purpose and be reintegrated with the people he will lead.

CHARACTERIZATION

The challenges and changes confronting Clemente Chávez control most of the action in this novel. In Albuquerque Clemente will be tested as father and husband; indeed, his very identity will be called into question. The alienating environment of the city and the condition of unemployment will lead him to drink and degradation. He will lose respect and authority within his family and arrive at the brink of total ruin. From the beginning he is the family member least able to adjust to the new environment.

His dependence on the land and the rituals of the past fail to acknowledge the potential of his new life in the city. Lacking the resources to prevent his own decline, he will reach the ultimate point of despair and even embrace the possibility of death before his "rebirth," assisted by Crispín (122). Clemente will emerge nevertheless, albeit reluctantly, as a community leader. His quest is not for personal power but, rather, is the result of an intense process of heightened social consciousness and cultural identification. (Several critics believe that the character is suggestive of and may in fact be Anaya's homage to the well-known Chicano labor organizer César Chávez.)

For Heiner Bus the character of Clemente represents a universal ideal:

In *Heart of Aztlán*, the defeated, once powerful individual is reconstructed in the context of an ethnic myth, with the assistance of the tribal bard [poet/singer], and the cooperation of the barrio people gradually acknowledging their common past, present, and future. . . . The Barelas concept of brotherhood and community is ethnic and regional, but it is also universal as an example of aspiration to social reorganization based on positive values and a meaningful reconciliation of past and present. ("Individual Versus Collective Identity" 126)

Others consider the character of Clemente unconvincing, moving through the novel with no direction until his moment of revelation. They question whether the reader can accept that all of Clemente's subsequent behavior is strictly based on his "vision" (Lewis, "Review" 76). For Cordelia Candelaria, all the characters of *Heart of Aztlán* are not realistically developed but are instead "*raza*** literary types" ("Rudolfo A. Anaya" 43) with little pretense of depth.

*"Raza" is literally translated as "the race"; it is used by Chicanos to refer to their ethnic/cultural group.

Jason Chávez is another main character in the novel. Like Clemente, Jason is one of the more developed characters and exhibits similar qualities. Jason also respects the land and the ancient customs of his people. He is portrayed as a sensitive young man who is open to the teachings of his elders (his friendship with the Indian in *Bless Me, Ultima* is mentioned in *Heart of Aztlán*, and he is portrayed as seeking similar guidance from the poet/seer Crispín). Similar to Clemente, Jason has leadership potential, in this case with the youth, having organized a local gang. The two heroes are usually portrayed in separate chapters, only appearing simultaneously in Chapters One, Two, Three, and Nineteen. Also like his father, Jason tends toward reintegration and unity; he understands such unusual characters as those in Willie's family and attempts to arbitrate between them and the other gang members. Finally, like Clemente, Jason must experience his own rites of passage, from adolescence into manhood, from his breakup with Cristina to the temptations and the physical dangers in the challenging environment of the Barelas barrio.

Crispín is a familiar character within the Anaya repertoire: the spiritual guide or mentor. In *Heart of Aztlán* this favorite Anaya character is portrayed as a barrio poet, a blind seer who sings the history and reality of the people and gives guidance. He teaches Clemente the meaning of the concept of Aztlán; and after saving Clemente's physical life he assists in his rebirth into a new spiritual one. As in the case of similar Anaya characters in other novels, Crispín possesses magical healing powers: his guitar can play life-giving music (recall the scene in which Frankie cheats death with the sounds of Crispín's blue guitar [196]).

Other characters in the novel are less developed and represent barrio social types: the unfeeling priest, the greedy businessman, the radical dissident. Certain Chávez family members also fall into this category: Benjie is a young, foolhardy victim of the dark side of pachuco culture, embodied by his own paralysis at the end; Juanita and Ana also flounder in this culture, becoming unskilled workers in a society that offers them few alternatives. The somewhat more complex female character of Clemente's loyal wife, Adelita (her name recalls that of the anonymous "Adelitas," or camp followers, who devotedly followed the troops during the Mexican Revolution of 1910–1920), is a strong mother figure who takes risks, is open to change for the betterment of her family, and stands faithfully at Clemente's side during his worst moments. She represents stability even as she recognizes the need for and helps to effect change within the domestic sphere. At the novel's end she will emerge from the domestic realm and join Clemente in the general social struggle for change, adapting once again as proves necessary.

ALTERNATIVE READING: A MARXIST VIEW OF *HEART OF AZTLÁN*

Although the German social philosopher Karl Marx (1818–1883) did not produce a systematic theory of art or literature, a body of criticism has emerged that is derived from the core of Marx's economic and political philosophies. Marxism holds a fundamental premise: that the history of society is a history of "class struggle," a battle between economic classes competing for power. In the capitalist economic system, the capitalist class—those who control the wealth, the financial institutions, and the means of producing the necessities of life—flourishes by extracting profits from the commodities produced by the working class. Economic demands shape the social relations among people; social inequality arises when those in control, who do little of the actual work, benefit from the labor of the workers who are usually inadequately compensated. As a result, the world that the workers themselves create does not belong to them but, rather, to those who exploit them. Marx condemned capitalist societies, believing that ultimately the working class would revolt against the inequalities and injustices of the system and seize control of the means of producing the wealth. He envisioned a classless society in the future, characterized by a more rational economic cooperation among its members, thus eliminating poverty and economic inequality.

Marxist literary criticism generally holds that literature is related to class and the economic conditions under which it was created; that truth is not eternal and unchanging, but institutionally created, a social practice like language itself; and that art is a commodity that is guided by these same social practices. This brand of criticism insists on a view of literature inseparable from other products of human activity or from history itself. For Marxist critics, art and literature reflect the inevitable class struggle of history and are the products of the cultures in which they originate.

A Marxist approach to *Heart of Aztlán*, then, focuses on the contradictions of an exploitative society. Anaya leaves no doubt as to who the exploiters are or their motive—economic gain. The historical forces that affect the characters' lives are the result of economic changes in society; the conflicts they confront are also largely based on material conditions created by the capitalist exploitation of the working class. The Chávez family is forced to leave their llano land, like many other families, as a result of socioeconomic factors; the beginning of their loss began long ago when the Anglo invaders/settlers took over the area and changed the laws to favor their own economic expansion. Among the changes the new settlers brought with them was barbed wire, the fencing in or privatization of property that prevented traditional cattle ranching on open plains. Few of the Hispano families could accommodate these economic and legal changes, which were created to benefit the Anglos.

With meager opportunities for economic survival, families were suddenly converted from small landowners (many had lived on the land for generations, benefiting from the original Spanish land grants and communal lands held for centuries) into members of the urban working class. The growth of urban centers in the 1940s was a beacon of hope for these families, hopes that were quickly dashed by the conditions they encountered in the rural ghettos they were forced to inhabit: inferior housing, precarious working conditions, racial and ethnic discrimination, lack of educational opportunity for their children, drugs and gang violence. Separated from their extended family and village networks, many lacked the reliable safety nets they had established back home. *Heart of Aztlán* examines the particular forms of exploitation that affect the Chicano working class of the novel: the anonymous technological giants of the railroad industry reflected in the corrupt puppet union leader, Kirk, the Catholic Church as represented by Father Cayo, and the capitalist business class in the form of the character of Mannie Garcia.

The main source of income for the men of Barelas is employment in the Santa Fe railroad yards. That no care is taken to protect the workers from exposure to dangerous working conditions is made clear from the beginning when a worker dies due to cutbacks that leave crews shorthanded. Stories of men losing fingers and limbs are tied to company neglect and to the corrupt union leaders who defend the interests of the owners over those of the union members. Although the railroad owners are not specifically mentioned by name, and although the author occasionally presents the industry in a mythical manner (for example, comparing the trains to serpents), Anaya leaves little doubt that the workers are exploited for economic reasons, and the "evil" that the railroad yard represents is of a very human kind based on monetary greed.

Father Cayo is a cynical priest who represents the Church, not as a spiritual entity, but as a social institution of power that is a vital player in the maintenance of the status quo. It is an ideological institution, part of the "superstructure" that, with the banks and the military, supports the dominant capitalist economic system. Father Cayo is clear on this point when he explicitly defines the Church's role to Clemente (142). According to Cayo, the Church ensures that the people will resign themselves to their poverty and abuse as a way of gaining eternal salvation. It is part of a hierarchy of power that maintains the social stability required by the capitalist system in order for it to survive and flourish; without the stability of the Church, the military, the financial institutions, and the moneyed classes, the entire system would collapse. Father Cayo clearly sees the role of the Church and its very survival as dependent on the continuation of things as they are, regardless of their negative effects on the Chicano working class.

The capitalist mentality at its worst is embodied in Mannie Garcia, who has learned how to manipulate the system to his best economic advantage, even as it destroys his faith in humanity. El Super has learned how to negotiate with the Anglo world and is not above some corruption of his own; *la mordida*, or the bribe, is a way of life he espouses. When asked to help his people, he adamantly refuses, spurning other Chicanos as "ungrateful scum" (153). Mannie is familiar with the intricacies of bank credit and profit, but he has lost his cultural identity, his soul. As Marx suggested, the focus on the attainment of money for its own sake does not necessarily make someone happy. It can drive a wedge between people, as demonstrated by el Super, who speaks of envy and distrust as natural outcomes of economic success; others will always envy those who succeed, he claims, and try to tear them down (154–155). He accuses Clemente of being a communist (154) and has alienated himself from his own community.

If art is indeed a symptom of social conditions, as Marxist critics hold, then *Heart of Aztlán* embodies the alienation and class conflicts that result from an exploitative system. The work exposes the corrosive effects of the Anglo capitalist system on Mexican Americans. Their disintegration is portrayed on an individual level—the poverty, drinking, and hopelessness of Clemente Chávez and his loss of authority and stability within the family—and on a societal level, as the workers are beaten down by their experiences, unable to defend their rights, paralyzed by powerful institutions and circumstances beyond their control. The initial step toward the utopian society envisioned by Karl Marx is not, however, the armed violence preached by the radical union leader Lalo; *Heart of Aztlán* advocates a change that starts from within, where the answers to the problems described must first be discovered.

Tortuga
(1979)

A traumatic experience during Anaya's adolescent years inspired the third novel of his New Mexico trilogy. One day while swimming with friends in an irrigation canal, Anaya dove in, hit bottom, and fractured two vertebrae in his neck (see chapter 1 in this book). He was paralyzed instantly. Saved from death by his friends, Anaya then had to undergo the painful process of physical therapy and healing. The fear and anguish he faced as a result of this event, and the solutions he forged to heal his battered body and tortured psyche, found their way into *Tortuga*. There the teenaged protagonist must conquer fear and doubt as he attempts to understand and overcome the limitations of his condition.

Linked to *Bless Me, Ultima* and *Heart of Aztlán* in the repetition of certain motifs and the extensive use of myth, symbolism, and dreams, *Tortuga* continues Anaya's message of healing and hope through self-awareness and the power of love.

NARRATIVE STRATEGIES

As in *Bless Me, Ultima, Tortuga* is narrated in the first person; in other works of this type the reader's perspective is limited to the point of view of the narrating voice. In this particular work, however, that point of view has specific physical limitations. From the first paragraph we are told that the protagonist is paralyzed; his range of vision is compromised by his body's restrictions. But although his viewpoint is impaired by physical obstacles, his mind is restless and questioning, analyzing all around him.

Yet the voice of the protagonist is not the only one we will hear in this novel. He will share the narration with another voice, that of Salomón, whose consciousness will eventually blend with his own. The young quadriplegic will be Tortuga's spiritual guide through the ordeals the hero must experience before reaching true understanding. Anaya's method for distinguishing between these two narrative voices is to differentiate the format of the text with italics, a method he had used extensively in *Bless Me, Ultima* and *Heart of Aztlán*. Italics in his previous novels were used to differentiate spacial/temporal levels of narration: in *Bless Me, Ultima* the protagonist's dreams were italicized, and in *Heart of Aztlán* mythical italicized sequences are interspersed throughout the novel. In *Tortuga* that distinction is reserved for Salomón's messages.

Dream sequences, a favorite device of Anaya, are integrated into the narration of *Tortuga* and fulfill the role of indexing the main character's interior evolution. Dreams demonstrate the subconscious dilemmas of the protagonist even as they forecast future events. Therefore, in *Tortuga* dreams serve several functions: structurally they act as a framework for the protagonist's development, and thematically they influence the outcome of events.

PLOT DEVELOPMENT

The first two chapters introduce the main characters of the entire work: from the drivers who transport the young patient, to the doctor, nurses, assistants, and other patients, we meet the majority of the characters who will have a profound effect on Tortuga's spiritual and physical quest. The setting for the story, also established in the introductory chapters, is a prisonlike hospital that faces a mountain shaped like a turtle; it will come to be identified with the protagonist himself.

Paralyzed as the result of a tragic event, the young protagonist Tortuga (Ben Chávez from *Heart of Aztlán* and *Alburquerque*) awakens from a restless sleep in an ambulance that is taking him deep into the dark, cold, desolate landscape of a colorless desert. Barely able to move his head, he can distinguish only the bare silhouette of a mountain range and a "diffused, distorted rainbow" in the sky (1). The rainbow recalls his childhood and his mother, for whom rainbows represent the mantle of the Virgin Mary. His mother's touch and her childhood rhymes had the power to heal him in his youth; her love cannot heal the trauma of his paralysis, though, which she rationalizes as "God's will" (2).

The first pages of the novel reveal the fact that the protagonist is a sixteen-year-old boy bound for a hospital in the south that specializes in the care of crippled children. That is where he can hope to regain the use of his limbs. The ambulance driver is a kindly old man, Filomón, who has made the journey many times before; his assistant, Clepo, is an "impish man with hunched shoulders" (2). Filomón acts as a guide, pointing out Tortuga Mountain to the boy, stopping the ambulance to better appreciate its wonder. Originally an Indian winter ceremonial ground due to its healing waters, the Spanish settlers had named the mountain's spring "Los Ojos de la Tortuga" (The Eyes of the Turtle) and the nearby village "Agua Bendita" (Holy Water). Filomón refers to it as a "magic mountain" rising so high it appears to "hold the heavens and the earth together," the sun glistening on the mountain after the rain covers it "with a sheen of silver" (3).

The main character sees little of this, however. He perceives only the outline of a turtle that gives the mountain its name. His experiences have left him weakened: "my faith in magic had drained out the night the paralysis came" (3). Filomón encourages the boy with optimism and hope. The storms they travel through will help the desert bloom in the spring, he says, and the trip they are taking is a "journey of life" (4). But for Clepo, crossing the desert is a "journey of death," perhaps a reference to the fact that the ambulance used to transport patients is indeed a converted hearse. He attempts to elicit the story behind his passenger's paralysis, but the boy reveals little: "since the paralysis the past didn't matter. It was as if everything had died, except the dream and the memories which kept haunting me" (4). Filomón is more hopeful; his passenger, he assures him, will improve by spring, when nature comes alive. He briefly touches the boy, who senses a strange healing force in the old man; Filomón once again repeats the message of the mountain's powers.

For the boy, however, the mountain is merely a reflection of his own feelings of hopelessness and alienation. He is unable at this point to perceive its underground rivers of healing "turtle pee." The mountain, he is told, was once a real sea turtle "which wandered north when the oceans dried and became deserts" and is now waiting for the earth to change again and liberate it. But Filomón's passenger is not yet prepared to understand this message. The boy perceives nature in harsher and less benign terms. He sees only a desert that is "wide and lifeless," burnt by a hard sun and winter whirlwinds that rise snakelike to the sky through pouring rains.

When their long trip is finally over, a new journey begins for the boy with his arrival at the hospital, a gloomy, stale, and dark place. Women are visiting their children, but the boy cannot expect visitors for himself. The poverty that paralyzes his family will not allow his mother to visit, and her prayers, he believes, will do him little good: "I had long ago lost the faith in my mother's gods" (8). A brief ray of hope enters his life when a beautiful young girl, the nurse's aide Ismelda, offers him a drink of mountain water. Her touch energizes him, and Filomón predicts that he will dream of her. She knows the mountain's healing secrets and is adept at folk remedies. When Ismelda leaves he briefly falls asleep and dreams of his mother's belief in God's will and his father's fatalistic views of man's inescapable destiny; he rejects both ideas.

The evaluation by his physician, Dr. Steel, leads to a body cast that, like a shell, will cover him from his hips to the top of his head. As the cast is created his mind wanders, and he begins to identify with the mountain, "safe in my new shell, safe as the mountain" (14). It is a safety that is short lived. The cast hardens and quickly becomes oppressive. In the dark room in which he lays he is visited by another patient, Danny. His visitor refers to him as "Tortuga" (Turtle), and the name sticks; indeed, it is the only name the character will have throughout the novel. Although Tortuga will meet other boys in the hospital during his stay, Danny is among the most disturbing. Suffering from a strange debilitating illness that began with the withering of his arm, Danny dismisses Filomón's hopeful message and attempts to harm Tortuga with a lighted match. Another patient, Mike, wheels himself into the room, however, and saves the boy from danger.

Tortuga will encounter many other patients in the ensuing chapters— the twisted, deformed girls who emerge only in the darkness, young boys with various types of deformities and illnesses—but none so important as Salomón, who is first introduced to Tortuga in a dream. Abandoned for hours by a careless orderly in an unmarked room, Tortuga observes the mountain that comes to life in his imagination. Musing on Filomón's message of the mountain's secret power, he falls into a troubled sleep. In his dream Ismelda joins the young girls of his past who had participated in his First Communion ceremony. She escorts him into the mountain's powerful rivers, holding him close to overcome his fears, and leads him to the shore, where he sees a "frail, angelic boy"—Salomón—who is surrounded by crippled children (22).

The italicized tale that follows is Salomón's first of many throughout the novel, as much message as story. He begins by saying that long ago he was a hunter, and the hunt led him to his destiny. He had abandoned his father's farming life to join a hunting tribe. His father's way of life was in tune with nature, on the *"path of the sun,"* but his young blood urged him to pursue the call of the hunt. An initiation rite would be his downfall, however. To become a full member he was to kill the first animal he encountered. Stripped of the amulet his father had given him by the jealous tribe leader, he comes across a giant turtle. The turtle had laid its eggs and was about to return to the water when the leader urges the boy to kill it. In fear he reluctantly severs the turtle's head, but the animal manages to overpower him and return to the safety of the river. Following this deed that will haunt him his whole life, he leaves the river and the tribe, unclean and *"smelling of death. . . . That night the bad dreams came, and then the paralysis"* (25).

This dream is Tortuga's first contact with Salomón and has a healing effect on his body. By the end of Chapter Two we get our first indication that Tortuga's arms and legs will eventually respond to treatment; the magic of his dreams will have a curative effect. It is now clear that the protagonist's physical healing will be linked to progressive changes in his spiritual and psychological evolution. By Chapter Three he has himself begun to identify with his mountain namesake, and his recovery appears to be at hand: "A strength had returned . . . thanks to the grace of the mountain and the strength of the girl in my dreams. . . . My first step toward freedom had come" (27). These remarks turn out to be premature, however. They anticipate a hopeful resolution for the reader, but the character will not reach his desired freedom quite yet.

After Mike finally discovers Tortuga left helpless and forgotten in a hospital room, the protagonist begins to meet the other patients who will comprise his world for the next several months and hears the first mention of Salomón's ward. It is the place where, Danny informs him, the "vegetables," children on life-sustaining devices, are kept. A nurse who was reprimanded for Tortuga's abandonment spitefully transfers him to Salomón's ward, an area feared and reviled by the other patients. The description of the ward in Chapter Five is ominous: the long, deep hall, forsaken and musty, filled with the iron lungs that sustain each individual patient, remind Tortuga of "strange caskets" with "thin skeletons" surrounded by ghostlike nurses. The silent, shrunken bodies of the patients are completely helpless save for their sad eyes, which follow him around the room. Tortuga's initial doubts as to the meaning of life are triggered by this visit, wondering why these helpless children are kept alive. The nurse escorts the horrified boy to Salomón's room, a private space earned by Salomón's longevity in the hospital. It is lined with books and magazines, small plants, and a window that faces Tortuga Mountain. Salomón is completely paralyzed except for his eyes, but he will communicate with Tortuga nevertheless.

The morphine administered by the nurse to calm the agitated patient brings on a second dream in which Tortuga again hears the words of Salomón. In spiritual communication with the boy, Salomón anticipates Tortuga's actions and anxieties; his messages are meant to inspire. The second dream establishes Salomón's most important lesson, one that will be repeated in one form or another throughout the novel: "*As we teach you to sing and to walk on the path of the sun the despair of the paralysis will lift, and you will make from what you've seen a new life, a new purpose*" (41). What ensues in the rest of the novel is basically the elaboration of this message. Tortuga will learn to "sing" about the sufferings he will encounter, and from this he will discover the purpose of his own ordeals.

Salomón's first lesson in the dream addresses the despair felt by those in their situation. Salomón's paralysis had led him to attempt suicide, and he too cursed God and life itself for his condition. A "miracle" changed his life, however. A giant butterfly poised itself on an opening created in his throat and "pollinated" him (42). Salomón sensed the tiny eggs coursing through his blood, creating a new life within: "*I felt the tiny little chrysalises ripening, gnawing through their shells and rising to my throat to seek their freedom!*" (42). His words are the beauty of their love; his message is the sacredness of all life.

Returned again to the regular ward, Tortuga begins to encounter other patients, other stories. Jerry is a Navajo Indian who awakens before dawn whispering a prayer to the sun in order to assure its return each day. Jerry's faith in the sun parallels his certainty that his grandfather will one day arrive to help him escape the confines of the hospital. Mike, whose legs were burned beyond help in an accidental fire that killed his mother and sisters, is the leader of the boys. Sadsack's polio caused his family to reject him. "Why me?" is the question they all ask, except for Mike, who has arrived at the conclusion that there are no answers and no one to blame: "Things just happen" (47).

Tortuga's telepathic communications with Salomón continue. The books Salomón sends him to read and his messages become stages in Tortuga's education/initiation. Ismelda and the woman she lives with, Josefa, also contribute to the education process. Josefa is a folk healer who works as an aide in the hospital; she reinforces the folk legends related to the mountain and its ancient healing powers during her visits with the young patients. Ismelda's and Josefa's visits are the boys' only ties to the world outside of the hospital. For Tortuga, Ismelda's role is increasingly more important as she becomes the link between his dreams and his experiences. She brings him home-cooked meals, the comfort foods of Hispanic culture, and she and Josefa work their herbal healing remedies on Tortuga and the other patients.

Dreams become an important element of Tortuga's cure. Ismelda is the woman of Tortuga's dreams, but she dreams of him as well. Her gentle touch stirs sexual feelings in him, urges that are also stimulated by KC, the robust physical therapist who threatens and teases the patients to motivate them through the painful therapy sessions. After Tortuga's first session the boys hold a small celebration, but Tortuga senses impending doom and has a strange dream. Someone is lost in the snowstorm outside and is headed for the hospital. In Tortuga's nightmare that person is La Llorona, the legendary wailing woman who had killed her own children and searches for others to destroy. She appears as a frightening figure about to make him her next victim. When he awakens Tortuga hears the sound of horses and someone calling outside in another language. Jerry says that his grandfather has come for him and escapes the hospital, heading toward the treacherous snow-covered mountain pass. A new patient is brought in the next day. While searching for Jerry in the snow-storm the search party had come across Buck, a cowboy. Jerry's body is later discovered, and a new story is added to Tortuga's growing list of experiences.

Memories of home blend with the hospital that is now his world. He begins to observe each patient's attempt to deal with his fate. As Danny's condition worsens, for example, he turns to religion. Danny sends for a jar of sand from the Sanctuary of Chimayó, believed to have miraculous healing powers. On Danny's arm, however, the sand only spreads the disease more quickly. The others laugh at his naïveté. God, they say, does not visit the hospital for fear of contracting polio. Danny takes their words literally, as he does those of a preacher who claims that Christ will return to free the patients whose hearts are open to him. As a result, Danny paves the way for Christ's visit by obtaining a surgical saw and cutting open all the patients' casts.

The days begin to blend into one another as Tortuga slowly recovers. Dreams of Ismelda and Salomón's messages draw Tortuga into a "complex web" (101). More than his physical recovery, Tortuga begins to concern himself with his destiny, the forces that will direct his life, his purpose. His search for such answers is not sustained by religious faith, however: "faith in the old powers was as dry as dust" (107). Mike's message regarding these ideas is simple and direct: "Get out! Escape! You owe it to yourself; you owe it to us!" (110). He warns Tortuga against complacency, noting that with few exceptions everyone concerned with the hospital is a former patient. Escaping its walls, crossing the desert, is too daunting for them. Tortuga must be different, though. As Mike tells him, "Salomón is betting on you" (111). The frequent mention of Salomón throughout the novel is associated with a message, a teaching, some sort of task.

In Chapter Fifteen Tortuga gets a wheelchair, but the happiness at his new mobility is tinged with a sense of foreboding: "*Come and see me when you can*, Salomón had said. . . . there's something you should see" (112). He wheels himself to Salomón's fearful ward, there to receive his instructions; he must face the dark, face his own fears, before he can find his song, which will be *"full of the sadness of life"* (117). Salomón compels Tortuga to enter the deepest and saddest of all the wards, where the pathetic sight of the comatose patients shocks him into despair. Everything he had accomplished up to this point loses meaning. Tortuga feels betrayed by Salomón, Ismelda, and the others for allowing him to penetrate such pain and hopelessness. He now feels only emptiness: "I was retreating, moving deeper and farther into my shell, covering my hurt and pain with layer after layer of silence . . . meaningless silence" (119). Angry and despondent after this experience, the protagonist withdraws into himself even as his cast begins to crumble around him. In a vulnerable state, Tortuga is led by Danny and his friends to the swimming pool, where they plunge him into the shocking water. Saved from drowning by Mike and the other patients, Tortuga's waterlogged cast dissolves, taking with it the dread and despair he had felt before.

Tortuga's dreams continue. In Chapter Nineteen he dreams of his First Communion ceremony on Easter Sunday, a ritual that filled him with questions. What was its meaning? Which sins could children his age possibly need to confess? The girls that shared his First Communion ceremony and now inhabit his dreams had aroused his sexuality. In Tortuga's dream their eager tongues accept giant white snow petals from the sky with the same anticipation as that of the white host from the priest's hands. The feelings they provoke in him cause him to run away and hide near the river (141).

This dream of sexual arousal and initiation is followed by an actual trip into town with the other adolescents of the hospital, where his dream will materialize. The outing is highly anticipated by all—it is their chance to be part of the outside world again and forget for a while their physical disabilities. Ironically, the objective of the trip is to see the movie *Frankenstein*. The young patients identify with the monster even as they take advantage of the darkened theater to ease their frustrated sexual desires. Cynthia, a girl plagued with serious physical deformities, reaches out to Tortuga, and they both express a needful love. As he touches her he fantasizes about the First Communion girls and Ismelda, confusing them in his thoughts. He returns to the hospital full of the joy of love and listening to "the song forming in my dreams" (157).

Tortuga's song will now find an instrument of expression. Spring has arrived, and his physical progress hints at the fact that he will soon be leaving for home. Ismelda confides her love for him and promises to wait for his return. A package from his mother informs him of labor problems back home among the workers and the death of Crispín (the poet/seer character from *Heart of Aztlán*). Crispín has left Tortuga his blue guitar, requesting that it be sent to him immediately. Struck by the fact that Salomón had predicted this outcome (thus the references to Tortuga's "singing"), his astonishment soon turns to frustration and anger. With a shattered left hand, how would he learn to play this instrument? The gift seems only to reinforce his impediment. He heads for Salomón's room, which he discovers is "stale and musty as a crypt," shadowed by Danny (170). Tortuga confronts Salomón with his predicament, but as usual Salomón's words lead him from despair to hope: "I swore that I would learn to draw the soul out of the blue guitar and learn to sing" (173). He will discover the words to tell their stories.

Chapter Twenty-Three begins with a sense of foreboding; Tortuga knows somehow that more sad verses will be sung. Meanwhile, the other patients congratulate him on his impending release from the hospital and plan a secret swimming party. That evening they gather at the pool, leaving behind the image of their twisted bodies and becoming "graceful golden mermen and mermaids" as they make love in the quiet waters (180). Their joy will be short lived, however. That same evening Danny pulls the electric switch, cutting power to the iron-lung patients—including Salomón—causing their deaths; he then cuts off his arm with a surgical saw.

Tortuga's final dream follows Salomón's death. In it he is accompanied by Ismelda and his other friends from the ward. They abandon their crutches, braces, and wheelchairs, gathering around Ismelda and Josefa to dance and sing and climb the mountain together. Everyone is there, including Jerry and Salomón. At the summit they perform a May dance around a juniper tree. Then the mountain itself joins in the dance, breaking free from the earth where the screams of the people below fill the darkness. The mountain floats into the solar system, and Tortuga and his friends also rise to become a "glowing sun" in the starry sky (187).

The following day as Tortuga prepares to depart, he slowly discovers that all of his friends had shared the same liberating dream. Before taking the bus that will return him north to his home, he stops to visit Ismelda. She too had shared the dream, and together they make love near the river, in view of Tortuga Mountain. On the bus for home (the bus driver resembles Filomón) Tortuga is accompanied by the blue guitar and Salomón's whispered message, now a part of his own consciousness, rejoicing in Tortuga's journey and his song of love (196–197).

CHARACTERIZATION

A clue to Tortuga's origins as a character lies in Anaya's second novel, *Heart of Aztlán*. Toward the end of that novel the protagonist's son, Benjie Chávez, is shot in the left hand and falls from a water tank, leaving him paralyzed. Further indications can be found in the reference to Crispín, the old man who bequeaths Tortuga his blue guitar, also an important character in *Heart of Aztlán*, and in the allusions to the "battle" of the working people back home in the letter from Tortuga's mother (168), itself a reference to the violence of the striking railroad workers in Anaya's second novel (see chapter 4 in this book). One need not have read Anaya's prior novels, however, to appreciate the world created in *Tortuga*.

As first-person narrator and main character, the reader hears Tortuga's reactions and observes experiences through his perspective. The hopes, flaws, and contradictions of a sixteen-year-old facing the challenges of healing himself physically and spiritually are narrated in a style that often gives the impression of someone much older than his years. One gets the impression that what is narrated are the remembered experiences of a mature adult, particularly in the more reflexive passages and the communications with Salomón. The style and tone of Tortuga's musings and Salomón's messages reflect Anaya's prose style, which in *Tortuga* (as in his earlier works) relies heavily on symbol and myth combined with a moral message. Anaya's protagonists must often undergo a mythical initiation of one type or another, and Tortuga is no exception.

Indeed, *Tortuga* follows a classic plotline of initiation and transformation: a character retreats to an isolated space, and after undergoing some sort of meditation, apprenticeship, and/or ritual or ordeal this character achieves enlightenment. Juan Bruce-Novoa notes, however, that Anaya takes the classic hero figure one step further: the hero in *Tortuga* raises not only his own consciousness but that of his community as well, "in order to lead the community into a higher realm of existence, one in which the essential, transcendent order of being can be recognized and followed in daily life" ("Author as Communal Hero" 193). Tortuga will fulfill his destiny as singer of their shared communal stories of human suffering and regeneration.

From the beginning of the novel the reader is given indications that Tortuga's journey will be a mythical one. The hero's pilgrimage from north to south through the desert of New Mexico takes place in a converted hearse/ambulance driven by old Filomón, a counterpart of Charon in ancient mythology, who rowed souls across the river Styx, the river of death. In the course of his cure Tortuga becomes the avatar, or embodiment, of a sacred mountain because of the similarity in shape created by his hard-shelled cast. "Buried" within his cast he is sheltered from the outside world and escapes frequently within himself for the personal reflections that will lead to his eventual release, his ability to crack the protective but confining shell. The hospital in which he abides, often described as a sort of prison, is also a labyrinth; he must make his way through its hellish wards to face his interior demons. That the hospital is no ordinary space is underlined by the primordial descriptions of the natural world that surrounds it: a pounding, unforgiving desert and a sacred mountain with healing underground springs.

Crucial to Tortuga's developing character is that of Salomón, mentor and protector of sacred spaces. A "disembodied" voice more than a flesh-and-blood character, his communications are like that of an oracle. Tortuga's voice and Salomón's voice approach each other tentatively at first, then increasingly more as the novel progresses until, by the end, they become as one. Like the wise old King Solomon of the Bible, Salomón is teacher and sage, despite his young age and physical limitations. He holds a privileged space in the "vegetable patch" of crippled children, seen by only those who dare to penetrate the frightening center of the hospital labyrinth. His philosophical tenet is to follow the "path of the sun," a solar theology of transformation: mankind, transformed into a new sun, can shine on new worlds. His ideas reflect a belief in the oneness of all things, a search for harmony, essence, and illumination. Although his name is associated with a biblical king, his nickname, "Sol," it should be noted, means "sun" in Spanish.

Salomón is Tortuga's spiritual shaman or guide. He will steer Tortuga from a symbolic death—the despair and rejection of life he experiences after entering the deepest ward of the hospital, as well as allowing himself to be thrown into the pool to drown—to a rebirth from the waters and the casting off of his shell/self. Salomón's lessons begin with his own story, his own process of spiritual confusion, regeneration, and illumination. The hunter who fell from grace must discover his own path from despair. The heroes of the past cannot provide the answers, he says, nor can one ascribe one's problems to an *"absent god. . . . Our own hero must be born out of this wasteland"* (159–160). Salomón's epiphany, or moment of illumination, is occasioned by his contact with nature; a humble butterfly reveals the essence and harmony of all creation to the crippled child.

Salomón's messages instruct Tortuga at crucial moments. They explain events and prepare Tortuga for his future role. By the end of the novel, Tortuga need not recur to Salomón's messages, for his friend's teachings have been internally assimilated so that Tortuga can now anticipate what Salomón might have said. On his way home at last, Tortuga tries to make sense of his experiences and wonders what may lie ahead for him. Salomón's whispered message responds. He is part of Tortuga now, despite the fact that he is only a memory.

Tortuga has been criticized for lacking some of the essential elements of story interest, among them well-developed characterization. Little is known of the main character that would make him more well rounded. Background information is sparse, the cause of his paralysis is unknown, and few facts can be gleaned outside of an impoverished family and a religious mother. The reader craves for more facts. Salomón is hardly a convincing character either; he is more voice/spirit than actual physical person.

Other characters are important to the plot and thematic development but are even less evolved. Danny, for example, is a shadowy character whose withered arm might be said to represent the tenacity of evil. Obsessed with himself and his problems, oblivious to the pain of others,

Danny is a fanatic; he believes in things literally and is unable to respond to subtlety or even the most basic human contact. Danny assumes that his suffering has significance and believes, therefore, that it is a punishment from God. He disparages mythic beliefs in the sacred mountain as nonsense, and his feelings of hate and envy drive him to commit terrible atrocities against himself and others. Mike is the voice of reason in the group, and his goals are more limited than those of either Tortuga or Salomón: he simply advises, "Get out!" He no longer seeks an explanation to tragic events, and he will not follow Salomón's teachings because he cannot make that type of commitment. A born leader, astute and compassionate, he has nonetheless lost faith in anything outside of himself and the world around him. He cannot transcend the world of material reality and take the spiritual leap.

Ismelda's character is of symbolic value: she is the ideal woman, pure feminine beauty and love. A character type repeated often in Anaya's works, Ismelda is a *curandera* (healer). She is a mysterious and magical figure, associated in Tortuga's mind with nature; she represents all the women of his past—she is the "lizard woman" who is both mother figure and lover. Ismelda will guide Tortuga toward Salomón and his journey of initiation, the outset of which is his very first dream. She is a mediator, a link between the world of nature and the supernatural; as a woman and his romantic ideal, she is Tortuga's inspiration. Through Ismelda and Salomón, Tortuga learns the curative and redemptive power of love. (It should be noted here that *Tortuga* has been criticized for exhibiting a *machista* attitude toward females. "Machista" derives from the Spanish words *macho* and *machismo*, a cultural value based on an exaggerated and aggressive masculinity. The banter among the teenaged male characters occasionally describes young girls in a derogatory, sexist manner that glorifies male dominance. On the other hand, the fact that there are tender love scenes between partners who might be rejected by the outside world for their physical deformities portrays a more open and liberating attitude toward sex, not bound by cultural stereotypes.)

As we have seen, the names of the main characters of Tortuga and Salomón are significant. Other characters' names are symbolic of their role or condition as well: Mudo (mute), Ronco (hoarse), Tuerto (one-eyed), and Sadsack are all nicknames that describe a malady or personality trait. The name of the hospital surgeon, Dr. Steel, is an allusion to the steel pins he uses to reconnect shattered bones and the fact that he is the true strength that sustains the hospital. Steel is a compassionate healer who sides with the patients and understands their pain.

THEMES

Like *Bless Me, Ultima* and *Heart of Aztlán*, *Tortuga* is constructed around
the motif of the mythic journey or quest. The protagonists in Anaya's
trilogy of novels experience rites of passage that lead them to a higher
state of consciousness or wisdom. The protagonist of *Tortuga* evolves
from a tortured, unremarkable boy into a thoughtful, spiritual, and compassionate young man who has considered the arguments of contrasting
creeds, taken the measure of good and evil, and developed a knowledge
of himself and the universe. Often compared to Thomas Mann's *The
Magic Mountain* (1924) for its similar plot and theme (in Mann's work a
young man spends seven years in a Swiss sanatorium and is radically
changed by his experience), *Tortuga* is a less ambitious work and culturally specific. From the title of the novel to the names of characters, the
references to foods, the places and traditions in the Spanish language,
the work is rooted within Hispanic culture, although that fact is not
specifically mentioned. Like *The Magic Mountain*, *Tortuga* is a philosophical novel to some degree, but Anaya is more focused on emotions; he
would convey his message through the heart.

The quest for self-insight is a basic theme of *Tortuga*. Presented as a
process that is the expression of a creative force, the main character must
develop the faculty gradually to arrive at self-fulfillment. *Tortuga* goes a
step further, however; the protagonist's self-fulfillment is contingent
upon his responsibility to community. His "destiny" will be fulfilled
when he "sings" or narrates the stories—the trials, sufferings, and joys—
of his people. Anaya has attempted to broaden the traditional coming-
of-age novel with philosophical, psychological, and mythological details.
The theme is couched in the artistic framework of dreams and spiritual
messages, which are forms of inner dialogues and conversations. Everything—plot, characters, conflicts—relates to the theme of self-awareness
depicted in the novel as a quest for the "path of the sun," the universal
harmony bonded in love.

Other themes can be ascribed to the work as well. The mythic vision
in many of Anaya's novels serves as a contrast to mainstream Anglo-
American culture. Within that context, when the folk and Native-
American traditions of healing and spirituality are compared in *Tortuga*
to conventional Anglo medical technology and institutionalized religions, the latter come up short. Tortuga and the other patients are healed
more by Josefa's and Ismelda's natural folk remedies, their "strong med-

icine" (9), than by the hospital's sterile approach. Though Tortuga had long ago lost faith in his "mother's gods," he could still be inspired by a cosmic vision of natural harmony. *Tortuga*'s critique of institutional medicine and religion does not necessarily call for a total elimination of those traditions. Rather, it invites the reader to consider the power of alternative traditions that are compatible and valuable.

The deformities of the patients act as a metaphor for the unequal value systems Tortuga must learn to distinguish: good and bad, beautiful and ugly, rich and poor—the protagonist must differentiate authentic from inauthentic values and not be misled by outward appearances or stereotypes. Despite his love for the beautiful Ismelda, for example, Tortuga will learn that his feelings for the hunchbacked Cynthia are also valuable as he takes another step in his moral maturity.

The metaphor of illness can be extended even more. It is logical to ask, for example, just exactly what Tortuga's song will be about. The immobility of the hospital community (that of the patients, as well as that of the rigid hospital bureaucracy) extends to the outside community. The metaphor can be understood as a reference to the larger Hispanic community, inactive and paralyzed in the face of overwhelming social problems. In that regard the singer as healer metaphor (in some Native-American traditions "singer" and "healer" are interchangeable words) can be considered a call to social action, to mobilization, an awakening to social consciousness from a dangerous, life-threatening state of unconsciousness.

ALTERNATIVE READING: MYTH CRITICISM

The emphasis on dreams in the psychic development of the protagonist in *Tortuga* and the archetypal qualities of many of the characters—Tortuga, Salomón, Danny, and Ismelda in particular—lend themselves to an analysis based on myth literary criticism (discussed in chapter 3 herein) in which varying methods and disciplines converge. We will look at *Tortuga* as a reflection of Anaya's mythic vision (see chapter 2 herein), which has been influenced by psychiatrist Carl Jung's theories regarding universal or archetypal principles.

As in *Bless Me, Ultima*, the protagonist of *Tortuga* is also a boy-hero who must complete the rite of passage of separation, initiation, and return. From his pilgrimage through the desert, driven by a counterpart of the mythic Charon, to his "burial" in a cast that will force him to

travel a world within himself, the hero will face the challenges of a spiritual initiation and a symbolic death and rebirth in the labyrinth of the
hospital before he can realize his quest and safely return.

The protagonist is identified with a mountain, a symbol of spiritual
elevation, the peak of illumination. Nature and landscape play important
roles in Anaya's writings (see chapter 2 in this book); in *Tortuga* the
relationship between humans and nature also reflects Anaya's mythological vision: "The gods come from the sea and the trees and the mountains and the caves and the forest, and people responding to those
landscapes are responding to those gods. . . . Different landscapes give
rise to a different form of gods and demons" (Jussawalla and Dasenbrock, *Interviews* 252). The setting for *Tortuga* denotes its mythical framework: a punishing desert, a magical mountain, sacred rivers with
mysterious internal caves, and a healing, illuminating solar system form
the background that gives rise to the particular types of gods and demons in Anaya's novel.

Following Jungian archetypal analysis, Ismelda would personify the
Anima, or feminine principle, the eternal feminine force. The protagonist
refers to her as all the women he had ever known before. Moral guide
and nurturer, she represents ideal womanhood. Danny, on the other
hand, represents the destructive, negative force of the archetypal
Shadow. Indeed, Danny does shadow Tortuga, lurking around, observing his movements. Like a shadow in darkness, Danny is incapable of
absorbing positive illuminating messages and is intent on preventing
others from doing so. Salomón's teachings are so much gibberish to
Danny, who eliminates the message even as he destroys the messenger.

Salomón can be compared to the Jungian archetype of the divine child,
the formative forces of the unconscious from which emerge wisdom and
understanding. A mythic child who is immobile save for his eyes, Salomón is illumination itself, as his nickname, Sol, implies. First introduced
to Tortuga in a dream, Salomón will also experience a type of death and
rebirth that parallels Tortuga's. A crippled child who has despaired and
attempted suicide, he is regenerated by an epiphany with nature (the
butterfly) and will be reborn in Tortuga. Their identities mesh at the end,
resulting in a type of reincarnation for Salomón and a revelation for
Tortuga, who finally achieves his integrated self.

The mechanism by which Tortuga's personality achieves integration
reveals itself in his dreams: the communication between the unconscious
and the conscious. For Jung, dreams reveal messages of a personal and
collective nature that, when assimilated, produce psychic development.

Tortuga's dreams are mythic. In his first dream he will meet his spiritual shaman, Salomón, the master of his destiny, as he plunges into his unconscious, symbolized by his descent, guided by Ismelda, into the sacred rivers of Tortuga Mountain. Purified by the waters and escorted by the Anima, he meets with the Self who relates the first of many sacred messages. The dreams that follow chart further stages of his individual development in a spiral progression until his final dream, which projects the protagonist and the other characters upward to the top of the mountain. This common or communal dream is the culmination of the hero's mythic journey; he and the others rise like "glowing suns" into the cosmos, thus completing his mystical initiation and redemption. Healed and transformed, the hero is now finally deserving of his destiny, worthy of the role he has been called upon to play.

Alburquerque
(1992)

The spelling of the title of Rudolfo Anaya's 1992 novel is based on a New Mexican legend, as explained in a foreword to the work. In 1880 an Anglo stationmaster reportedly dropped the "r" from the original name of the city because he could not pronounce the word, a move that symbolizes for Anaya the emasculation of the Mexican way of life. *Alburquerque* restores the city's original name even as it addresses other historical events that have left their mark on the U.S. Southwest and continue to effect changes there today. As is customary in Anaya's fiction, the novel revisits several characters from his earlier works and introduces a new set of characters, several of whom will figure prominently in later works. Sonny Baca, for example, a minor character in *Alburquerque*, will be the protagonist of Anaya's detective novels *Zia Summer, Rio Grande Fall*, and *Shaman Winter*.

Alburquerque is a departure from Anaya's earlier fiction in both setting and tone: it is a more contemporary story with less emphasis on mystical themes and symbols and a more accessible style. Nevertheless, the novel expresses Anaya's ongoing concerns: the preservation of communal relationships that have sustained traditional cultures for centuries, the pernicious rise of materialism, and the classic struggle between good and evil. "We, the writers, cannot wait out the storm; we have to confront it. For us, the bedrock of beliefs of the old cultures provides our connection, our relationship. From that stance we must keep informing the public about the change that has come upon our land" ("Mythical Dimensions" 351).

POINT OF VIEW

Largely told from the perspective of an omniscient, third-person narrator, *Alburquerque* presents several points of view as it weaves its complex plot. The main story involves the quest of Abrán González to discover the identity of his biological father, but this is not the only story. As the novel develops, other subplots, the perspectives of other characters, blend with that of the omniscient narrating voice. In the pages that contain italicized passages from Cynthia Johnson's diary, for example (94–106), the events are presented from her perspective in a voice we had heard briefly before in an earlier scene, during Abrán González's visit to his dying mother in the hospital (25–26). The other narrating voice heard on occasion is that of Cynthia's father, Walter Johnson, who relates the experiences of his arrival and successes in New Mexico from his own point of view (43, 225–226). This presents a contrasting Anglo perspective to a story that generally empathizes with a Hispanic/Native-American version of historical events.

LANGUAGE

As in other Anaya novels, the author here intersperses words and expressions from the Spanish language, frequently defining their meaning for non-Spanish speakers. Words that are not defined or repeated in English are not indispensable to an understanding of the novel, however, although an appreciation of Spanish does privilege the bilingual reader. Anaya wishes to create an authentic local atmosphere in his novels, and language is, of course, an integral component of the sociocultural reality he portrays. But the issue of language goes beyond tone to a thematic concern: the idea of acceptance into certain social circles revolves around the use of language. For the character of Abrán to be accepted as a genuine Chicano, he had to speak a *barrio* Spanish (21) to prove his "Mexicanness," and political figures like Frank Dominic benefit from a knowledge of the Spanish language and culture as they attempt to earn the Hispanic vote. Thus, language is both a badge and a weapon in this book.

PLOT DEVELOPMENT

Alburquerque has been referred to as a plot-driven novel; Anaya presents a complexity of events in the form of many plot threads which the reader must tie together to grasp the final pattern. Although the major story is ostensibly Abrán González's search for his biological father, the novel shifts from one angle to the next without always satisfying the reader's curiosity about the characters or their lives. The tension of the reader's anticipation and curiosity as to the outcome of Abrán's quest is quickly dispelled—the author reveals Abrán's father's identity early on in the novel. The use of converging plotlines that move toward one another, the reader soon discovers, reveals the fact that the main story of *Alburquerque* is not really Abrán's quest at all, but a wide-reaching tale of history, ambition, and greed and their effects on the people of New Mexico.

In the first chapter we are introduced to Ben Chávez, an author and professor at the local university and a regular at Jack's Cantina, an old hangout. Ben is working on a story about the current political situation, the mayoral race between Frank Dominic, his high school friend, and the incumbent, the beautiful Marisa Martínez. Both would like his support in their campaigns, but Ben has other thoughts on his mind: a story that "he has never told" (2) about Cynthia, who now lays dying of cancer in the hospital.

Fat Bernie, a bully from Ben's high school days in the barrio, challenges him to a pool game for money. The stakes rise as Ben shows he can surpass Bernie's talent at the game. A crowd gathers to watch a winning Ben inadvertently touch the eight ball with the back of his cue stick. Bernie and his friend Chango take advantage of the mistake to attack Ben and begin a fight, reminding Ben of the old times in the barrio when one had to fight to defend one's place (5).

Chango draws a switchblade but is warned to put it away by Joe Calabasa, a Native-American Vietnam veteran who enters the bar with Abrán González, a former Golden Gloves boxing champion. Joe and Abrán fight the aggressors off and drive the injured Ben home. On their way out of the bar Ben catches a glimpse of a dead snake, reminding him of the Zuni snake dances; the dead serpent, he muses, is a bad omen. The descriptions of nature here are also ominous, with spring windstorms riding the souls of the dead (8). Ben's encounter with the young men seems to be predetermined; he senses that they were destined to meet. Ben had already met Joe in one of his university classes; Abrán is known to him by reputation.

Upon reaching their destination, the young men enter the writer's home, where Joe notices a large painting on the wall, a depiction of a traditional *matanza*, or hog butchering. Ben returns a handkerchief he had borrowed from Abrán to clean his wound, and as the men ride away Ben reflects again on Cynthia in the hospital. It is springtime, a time of "transition" and "awakening." Ben's reflections are a foreshadowing, or a hint of what is yet to come: old issues that must be resolved from a past that refuses to die (10).

On the way home from Ben's house Joe and Abrán discuss changes in the city, including the candidacy of Frank Dominic, who has development schemes that involve the water and land rights of the native peoples in the area. Joe had distanced himself from his people in his pueblo after his traumatic experience in Vietnam left him with a drinking problem. He is now trying to find a way back to his roots and his traditions. Abrán understands his friend's pain. He feels remorse for causing the accidental death of one of his other friends, Junior Gómez, after one of their sparring sessions; the death of his own father, Ramiro, has also affected him deeply.

Joe and Abrán separate, and Abrán heads for his mother's home in the Barelas barrio. The familiar aromas of Mexican foods greet Abrán as he notices a letter from the hospital addressed to him. It is a letter that Sara, his mother, has dreaded for years. The message, sent by a woman wishing to see him and claiming to be his mother—Cynthia Johnson—finally forces Sara to tell Abrán that he is adopted. Abrán receives the news with shock but not total surprise. As a child he noticed that he did not resemble either of his parents; his skin and hair were lighter, his features were different. The neighbors referred to him as a güerito, or fair skinned. But Cynthia Johnson was a famous artist, the daughter of a wealthy and prominent banker. How could she be his biological mother?

Sara patiently explains that Abrán was given to her husband and herself as a baby. They worked for the Johnson family, and when Cynthia, called Cindy by her friends, got pregnant in high school her father demanded that she terminate the pregnancy. Cynthia refused and gave up the child. All involved vowed never to reveal the truth. When Abrán asks who his father is, however, Sara responds that she was never told his identity. The story leaves Abrán with grave doubts and anger. Driving to the hospital, he reflects on his mother's revelations and recalls his upbringing. As a young boy he had been forced to prove his "Mexican-ness" because of his fair skin. He spoke a barrio Spanish and used his fists to gain respect. Deep in thought he skids to avoid an old woman who runs in front of his car. With her wild hair flowing around a wrinkled face, he is reminded of La Llorona, the legendary wailing woman of folklore. The woman is actually Doña Tules, an old *curandera* (healer) who some believe to be a witch. She recognizes him and sends him a chilling message: "Your mother is dying, and you are being born" (23). She tells him to come to her when he wishes to know the truth and, pointing a finger at him, says, "Tú eres tú" (You are you) before crying off into the night (23). Her words perplex him even more.

At the hospital it is long past visiting hours, but a helpful nurse, Lucinda Córdova, takes him to Cynthia's room. Close to death, Cynthia responds to his touch, and when she coughs Abrán touches the same handkerchief to her lips that he had earlier used to wipe Ben Chávez's blood (we will later understand that this gesture unknowingly unites his biological mother and father). Cynthia dies soon after, never able to disclose his father's identity and leaving Abrán feeling cheated, not understanding why she had kept the secret so long (27). Indeed, the novel will begin to unravel many secrets of the past that the characters have been obliged, in one way or another, to maintain.

Following the old customs, Lucinda sits and prays at Abrán's side for the rest of the evening. The light of day reminds Abrán of Ramiro's words to him as a child. His father would speak to him of the power of the sun and teach him the ways of the ancestors. But who were Abrán's true ancestors? Knowing now that his mother was Anglo and convinced that his father was Mexican, what did that make him? A small, dark, handsome woman walks into the room and sobs over Cynthia's body. It is Vera Johnson, Cynthia's estranged mother. She begs Abrán's forgiveness and tells him as much as she can of his origins. Vera confirms Sara's story, adding that Abrán's father was indeed Mexican, a boy from the barrio, but she can tell him no more. Vera hands Abrán a diary left to him by his mother containing instructions for her burial.

In Chapter Three Abrán drives from the Barelas barrio to the "Country Club district" of the city, a distance that spans the poorest to the wealthiest neighborhoods of Albuquerque. The city is split economically and ethnically: the Chicanos live along the valley, and the Anglos inhabit the Heights. Strict rules of division maintain these socioeconomic borders. Abrán reflects that he himself is a child of those borders, of the separation

between whites and browns. Those born at the juncture of the barrier—
that is, those of mixed heritages and cultures—are referred to by his
people as "coyotes" (38).

Abrán finds Walter Johnson in his luxurious home, sitting imperiously
behind his desk. Vera has told Walter of his daughter's death, but he
wants nothing to do with the child he had given away years before.
Convinced that Abrán is there to obtain money, he is about to offer some
when the young man demands to know his father's identity. Walter is
unable to respond because he had never bothered to find out. Rejecting
Walter's offer of money, Abrán leaves, feeling only contempt for the man
who had made him an orphan.

Abrán's visit prompts Walter's memories of a past that refuses to "stay
buried" (41). He recalls the early years of his marriage and his reasons
for coming to New Mexico. The Depression and his tuberculosis forced
him to leave Chicago for his health; the desert air would restore him,
the doctors had said. Headed for California, he got as far as Albuquerque, barely alive. There he fainted in Don Manuel Armijo's cantina and
was restored to health, thanks to the loving care of Vera, an orphan girl
raised by Don Manuel and his wife. After a while Walter discovered that
Vera had a Jewish heritage. Her family were *marranos*, Spanish Jews who
had converted to Catholicism to begin a new life in the Americas. Old
documents showed that one of her ancestors, a Jewish sailor, had re-
nounced his heritage and sailed to the New World a reborn man. Walter
Johnson identified with the story of Vera's ancestors. He too had re-
created his past, a life of poverty and deprivation in Chicago, to start a
new existence in a new land. His rebirth began with his name. Upon
awakening in Don Manuel's cantina and asked by Vera, "¿Cómo te lla-
mas?" (What is your name?), he quickly invented a new one: he would
be known as Walter Johnson in this land of his rebirth, where he would
start a new life with Vera, another outcast, at his side.

Meanwhile, Abrán quickly discovers that Cynthia's diary contains little information regarding his father—no names, no details. In fact, the
diary relates little more than a lyrical description of a matanza she had
attended with his father. Disappointed, he decides to meet his friend Joe.
Half Santo Domingo Indian and half Mexican, Joe is another coyote, like
himself. But Joe's hardships in Vietnam have alienated him from his
people. Contrasting his Vietnam War experiences with the hunting experiences he had shared with his pueblo, in which the hunter gained
strength from the animal as in prayer, it is clear that the hunt for enemies
in Vietnam was totally destructive. In a telling incident Joe was under

attack by the enemy and decided to lay in wait for his predator. Finally the man emerged from the bush—an old man who reminded Joe of his grandfather. Joe reacted by singing aloud a song his father had taught him, a chant for deer. The old man responded with his own song in Vietnamese. Seeing in this man, his attacker, the face of his own people, Joe found peace. Both men turned away, forsaking death and destruction, and Joe was thereafter finished with killing and war. "The old man had liberated me" (52).

In Chapter Four Lucinda suggests that she and Abrán visit the Sandia Mountains. Lucinda, we learn, was influenced to enter nursing by a curandera from her village in the north. Her father had been attacked by a bear, and Doña Agapita's traditional therapy restored him. Lucinda plans to return home someday and create a clinic for the local people, and she invites Abrán to visit her family, hinting at her desire for a serious relationship with him that she has felt since their first meeting. He is, she believes, "the man I have seen in my dreams" (58).

Frank Dominic, meanwhile, is campaigning for the mayoral race, with his plans for urban development that include a gambling casino and canals on the Rio Grande. In Chapter Five Ben Chávez is invited to one of Dominic's gatherings, and despite his reservations about Frank and his sadness over Cynthia's death, he puts aside an epic poem he is composing and decides to attend. Frank is running not only against Marisa Martínez but also against Walter Johnson; between the two men, Ben believes Frank to be the lesser evil because Walter had destroyed his daughter's life and robbed Ben of fatherhood. At this point the reader learns that Ben is indeed Abrán's father; he is Benjie from *Heart of Aztlán*, Cynthia's lover, and he had promised her never to divulge their secret.

The remainder of Chapter Five is a discussion of Albuquerque politics. The mayoral campaign reflects different perspectives on the future of the city. The present mayor, Marisa, is attempting to interest a Japanese banker, Akira Morino, in investing in a computer chip plant. Frank, a self-made man profiting from the boom in real estate, wants the city to be another Las Vegas. Walter Johnson represents the status quo, with the established Anglo business community on his side. In Ben's words, "Alburquerque is already many cities" (65). He laments the fact that there are too many immigrants who know little of the city's history and nothing of the traditional communities. The city has become a mass of class and ethnic lines, "Borders in our own backyard" (67).

Frank Dominic yearns to be associated with one of the city's more

illustrious ethnic groups, the descendants of the original Spanish conquistadors of New Mexico. With no actual family ties to the Spaniards,
Frank is nevertheless intent on creating the image of a Spanish legacy:
"many a nut in New Mexico had spent his life's earnings trying to find
his link to a Spanish family crest" (72). Unaware of Ben's ties to Abrán
González, Frank has devised a plan to enhance his political campaign.
Now that it has become known that Abrán is the son of the late artist
Cynthia, Frank will ask Abrán to box an exhibition fight to draw crowds
to his campaign effort. Unable to explain to Frank why the idea angers
him, Ben leaves Frank's party in disgust, more angry at himself than at
Frank for his own failings.

Chapter Six opens with Cynthia's funeral, where Frank introduces
himself to Abrán and asks him to meet with him for "Cynthia's sake."
Then Abrán carries out Cynthia's specific instructions for her burial. Accompanied by Vera, Joe, and Lucinda, he follows the map she had left
him to an old cottonwood tree in an isolated setting leading to a bower
where her ashes are to be buried. Unknowingly, Abrán buries the urn
at the precise spot where he had been conceived. The following day
Abrán and Lucinda meet with Frank in an imposing building he constructed after forcing the original residents off the site. According to
Lucinda, Frank Dominic's plans for Albuquerque will find the Hispanic
youth "rowing boats up and down canals that cover the land where they
used to live" (82). In his luxurious offices, protected by guard dogs and
surrounded by Cynthia's paintings, Frank strikes a bargain with Abrán.
Despite the fact that he had vowed never to fight again, Abrán agrees
to enter the ring provided that Frank uncovers the identity of his father.

In Chapter Eight, during a visit to his mother's house with Lucinda,
Abrán reads from Cynthia's diary. This chapter is almost entirely dedicated to the diary excerpt, presented in italics, describing the fiesta of
the matanza, which Cindy describes as the soul of her people, her
mother's Mexican heritage (94). Cynthia had devoted her art to portray-
ing the customs and traditions of the Hispanic people who were in
danger of extinction. During the fiesta, a ritualized celebration—the
slaughtering of the hogs for winter—becomes a challenge between the
older generation and the younger members of the family, urban profes-
sionals who have lost their ties to nature and have forgotten their
traditions.

Chapter Nine returns to Frank Dominic and his schemes for the mayoral race and the transformation of Albuquerque. A neighbor of the incumbent mayor, he lusts for her body and her political power from afar.

We learn that Frank had been in love with Cynthia during his high school years, but she rejected him. His marriage to a woman named Gloria was born more of expediency than affection: Gloria is an authentic descendant of the old Spanish families that Frank admires. He has big plans for the future. But he must first hire Sonny Baca, a young brash detective, to discover the identity of Abrán's father and any facts against Marisa Martínez that he can use against her.

In a televised meeting among Abrán (whose Golden Gloves fame attracts the press), the mayor, and Frank at his office, Abrán and Marisa meet for the first time. The mutual attraction is immediate. Frank has organized the occasion to announce his development scheme for the city, called the "El Dorado plan," which includes the approval of the aforementioned gambling sites and, more daringly, a canal system running through the city that will make Albuquerque the Venice of the desert, with ponds and lakes linked by a vast waterway (119). His plans for tourism in the city hit a snag, however, when he is reminded that the water rights to the Rio Grande Basin that he needs for his waterway belong to the Indian pueblos and the Hispanic villages of the north. Frank's response to this problem is simple: he will privatize the water rights, convinced that the Hispanic villagers and the Indian pueblos will sell the rights for a share in the profits.

Ben Chávez interprets the matter differently. If the Indian pueblos sell their rights, the traditional way of life they hold sacred will disappear, forcing them to work in menial jobs in the city's tourist industry: "The minute you become a tourist commodity, you die" (128), he asserts.

All the while, the attraction between Marisa and Abrán grows; Marisa invites him to her home that afternoon to see a painting by his mother. Their meeting leads to lovemaking by the pool, photographed from afar by Sonny Baca—photos that Frank will use against the mayor in his campaign. The lovemaking, in turn, complicates matters for Abrán, who is confused by his feelings for Marisa and those for Lucinda. His passion for Marisa is strong, but thoughts of Lucinda keep entering his mind; she can fill his "spiritual center" (147). Sara notices his dilemma and suggests he see Doña Tules, the same woman who helped Clemente Chávez during the railroad workers' strike portrayed in Anaya's *Heart of Aztlán* and the same woman Abrán had almost run down on his way to visit Cynthia in the hospital. Doña Tules, we learn, had also assisted Vera Johnson when she gave birth to Cynthia.

For the time being at least, Abrán does not act on his mother's advice, but instead, on Good Friday, goes with Lucinda to visit her family in

the mountains north of Albuquerque. On the way they stop to see Cynthia's attorney in Santa Fe to probate her will. As they are driving to the
attorney's office, Lucinda reflects on a prophetic nightmare she had on
the evening of Abrán's visit with Marisa. Unaware of their encounter,
Lucinda dreamt that Abrán was drowning and that a woman, whom she
interpreted as La Llorona, was fishing for him. The episode clarifies that
Lucinda is intuitive, a curandera like Doña Tules. Abrán's feelings for
her intensify, and he decides he wants to share his life with her.

Reaching Santa Fe, they meet with the attorney, Moises Lippman, who
is unable to shed any light on Abrán's quest. He does, however, inform
Abrán of his inheritance from Cynthia, which includes an adobe house
that Lucinda senses is full of "spirits" from the past that need to be put
to rest (159).

From there they continue on to the Sanctuary of Chimayó, a small
adobe church north of Santa Fe that is the site of pilgrimages for what
is believed to be its healing powers. There Lucinda shows Abrán an earth
floor filled with the healing soil thought to produce cures. She wipes it
on his hands and arms, predicting that he too will be a healer.

The couple finally arrive at the small village of Córdova and the home
of Lucinda's parents, Juan Oso and Esperanza. Her father is a *santero*, a
carver of wooden saints, an old tradition in the area. Before becoming a
santero he had been a rancher—that is, before he confronted the bear
that changed his life.

Chapter Fourteen then tells this story of Juan Oso and the bear that
nearly killed him. As a young man he became involved with a girl
thought to be the daughter of a witch. The girl's father, a fierce, bearlike
man, threatened him, but when Juan's father went to speak to the man,
the family had disappeared. The cabin they left behind was a fearful
place, "like the den of a bear," an area his own father advised him to
avoid. Years passed, Juan married another, and he ignored his father's
warnings by taking his cattle to the area to graze. One evening a female
bear stampeded his herd. He followed her into the forest, where a male
bear lay in wait. Although Juan shot at it, the animal had already torn
at his arm and had locked its jaws on his flesh. As the bear crushed him
in its arms, he stabbed it with his hunting knife. His life was saved by
his wife's dreams. Esperanza dreamt that he was drowning in blood,
and she therefore searched for and eventually found him in the mountains, near death; the massive bear had disappeared.

The experience transformed Juan forever; during his recuperation the
bear spirit entered him (169), and from that point on he was called Juan

"Oso" (Bear). He had entered the animal world and was a part of it. His transformation also changed his occupation; seeing life with different eyes, Juan Oso became a santero, carving the figures of saints out of wood as a livelihood and a vocation. Fascinated by Juan Oso's story, Abrán learns more about the family's roots in the area, a history that dates from the time of the original Indian pueblos and Hispanics in the region, long before the arrival of the U.S. Army stripped them of their lands. The time with Lucinda's family confirms Abrán's feelings: she is the woman with whom he will spend his life.

Lucinda and Abrán spend a peaceful week in the mountains, where Lucinda tells him of her recurring dream; in it she sees a clay doll, representing a storyteller, with her own face. The doll is surrounded by children, and Lucinda is convinced that the dream is telling her she is pregnant with Abrán's child (179). Their joy is interrupted by a visit from Casimiro, Frank Dominic's henchman, who threateningly demands that Abrán return to Albuquerque; he has broken training for the fight, and Frank is upset. The next day Abrán and Lucinda make their way back, stopping first to visit Doña Agapita, the old curandera who had influenced Lucinda's childhood and taught her the traditional healing arts. The woman interprets Doña Tules's message for him: it does not matter who his father is, she says. His destiny as a healer is more important.

In Chapter Sixteen the narrator describes the ancient Native-American communal tradition of preparing the land for planting—the hard work of repairing the *acequias* (irrigations ditches) and the blessing of the corn and *calabaza* (squash) seeds before placing them in the earth. Their prayers for rain and a fruitful harvest reflect two traditions: that of the native kachinas (Native-American godlike ancestral spirits) and that of the Catholic saints. As in earlier scenes in which the old Hispanos worry that the young are forgetting the customs of their people, the same fear exists in the Native-American pueblo. The city takes the younger generation away to a place where they are lost; the pueblo is their life source (184). Joe Calabasa is one such victim, and he overhears a comment to that effect when he attends a council meeting of his tribe in which the leaders are discussing Frank Dominic's plans for Albuquerque. The council is deciding whether it should sell the water rights, something that Joe adamantly rejects but that is supported by the young Indian attorneys. Joe has little say in the matter, however, for despite his recent attempts to reintegrate himself into his tribe, his distance from the group has made it difficult to reenter the pueblo circle.

The chapter ends with Abrán's visit to Frank's office, where they argue about the upcoming boxing event. Frank knows of Abrán's affair with the mayor and berates him for breaking training with "that little bitch you run around with" (196). Offended by his demeaning reference to Lucinda, Abrán reaches out to hit Frank when his two Doberman guard dogs run to their master's defense and clamp their fangs on Abrán's leg. Abrán is taken away from the scene, and an angry Frank swears revenge.

Unable to reach Lucinda by phone, Abrán heads for Doña Tules's house for answers to his apprehensions. Doña Tules, we are told, was betrayed by a man in her youth, a man who had left her pregnant before disappearing. The child was never seen again, leading to questions of whether she, like the folkloric La Llorona, had drowned the baby in the river. The barrio gradually adapted to her eccentric ways, and some would seek her remedies for love and health problems.

Doña Tules has been expecting Abrán's visit. She knew that he would eventually seek his roots, but she tells him his search is futile: all he needs to know is the person within himself. He appreciates her reply but is still dissatisfied. Doña Tules mentions that at the time that Cynthia was pregnant, a certain man of the barrio, Clemente Chávez, came to her for help, a man who shared Abrán's "aura." She is speaking of Ben Chávez's father, but Abrán is unable to see that connection and leaves her house baffled. He next heads for Lucinda's home, but her reaction to seeing him does not bring the peace he desires. Lucinda has received an anonymous phone call informing her of Abrán's unfaithfulness with Marisa. Hurt and angry, she feels she can no longer trust him and asks him to go. A despondent Abrán departs for the bar, where he runs into Ben Chávez.

Ben refers to the patrons of the bar as his "characters" and, indeed, several of them are. A poetry reading has been organized with Ben reciting from his own work, an epic poem narrating the story of Juan Chicaspatas and Al Penco, two Chicano homeboys in search of the mythic Aztlán (a reference to an actual poem written by Rudolfo Anaya; see the "Characterization" section below). These fictional characters come "alive" as the protagonists of the poem inhabit the reality of the scene. The fact is alluded to in many ways: Ben describes Juan and Al as his "favorite characters," his *hijos* (children), "figments of his imagination" (213). When Abrán asks if they are "for real," Ben replies, "As real as their story" (213). Juan and Al are not the only element of fantasy in the chapter. Doña Loneliness, Ben's ghostly companion, appears to Ben and accompanies him home.

Chapter Nineteen returns to Walter Johnson and his plans to become mayor of Albuquerque. He has invited the leading businessmen and politicians to his home to announce his candidacy, men who are beginning to distrust Frank Dominic's grandiose plans. The Spanish spoken by the waiters tending the reception reminds Walter of his wife, Vera, the woman whose vision of the future led to his power and wealth and a crypto-Jew who "goes to church at Old Town with her Spanish friends, but she dreams of Jerusalem" (225). The narration reverts to Walter's point of view here, recalling Vera's insistence that he buy up land considered worthless. Her business acumen and their hard work and sacrifices fulfilled his dreams, but when they wished to build their own home the neighbors in the elite community rejected them. The presence of Jews like Vera was not condoned by the Anglos. Don Manuel, the man who had raised Vera and helped Walter initially, solved the problem: he devised a fake genealogy for her. Vera needed a new bloodline, and this could be obtained by willing attorneys who would "rearrange" her family background (231). Thus a new baptismal certificate and a letter of genealogy made Vera an aristocratic Catholic, and the Johnson family was welcomed into the city's elite class (231).

Vera enters the room, and now she too reflects on the past. Originally named Elvira Aguirre Armijo, she recalls a childhood in which she was taunted by other children for being Jewish and later her loneliness and desperation to become a mother. The reader learns that secrets and lies surround Cynthia's birth, not only Abrán's. After being childless for so long and attempting every possible remedy, Vera finally went with Sara, who was then her maid, to visit Doña Tules. After examining her, Doña Tules informs Vera that the problem is not hers but her husband's. Resolving to have a child, Vera had heard of a new gynecologist in town, a caring, handsome man with whom Vera established a brief relationship. Shortly afterward Vera became pregnant, and eventually Cynthia was born. The chapter ends with another reference to social duplicity. Don Manuel and Doña Eufemia, the couple who had raised the orphaned Vera, held positions of power in the Hispanic community and were courted by politicians for their influence. But they too had to maintain pretenses, pretending to be Spanish and not Mexican in order to gain acceptance into Walter's social circle (242).

The remaining chapters revolve around Abrán's decision to box for Frank's political campaign, as he had promised, and his continuing quest to discover his father's identity. Moises Lippman calls Sara, suggesting that Abrán locate the painting of Cynthia's titled *La Matanza* (in Ben's home) as a clue to his father's identity. Meanwhile, after a drinking

binge, Joe awakens to discover that it is the day of the scheduled boxing
match and that he must see his friend. Unable to locate Abrán, Joe is
anxious to get to Albuquerque to enlist Lucinda's help. He spots his
cousin Sonny Baca's truck and climbs in, invoking his crafty friend, Coyote, the trickster spirit of Native-American folklore, dressed like a "pachuco from the 1940s," who accompanies Joe on a wild rampage across
the university campus to locate Lucinda before proceeding on to Sara's
house. There Joe hears the message from Lippman regarding the painting
of *La Matanza* Joe had seen at Ben Chávez's home. He quickly figures
out the truth and heads for Ben's home to confirm his suspicions; Ben
admits he is indeed Abrán's father, a secret he had kept in deference to
Cynthia. Now Joe must find Abrán and prevent the fight.

In Chapter Twenty-One both Lucinda and Joe rush to locate Abrán, in
hopes of stopping the match. Lucinda had visited Marisa the day before
to confront her about her relationship with Abrán; Marisa admitted to
making love with him but confessed that their affair had ended there.
Armed with the truth, Lucinda now heads for the town's convention
center to make her peace with Abrán, but a throng of people block her
way. Marisa helps her enter just as Joe barges his way into the building,
screaming to Lucinda that he has found Abrán's father and pointing to
Ben Chávez. At that moment he receives a blow on the head by a police
officer, but as he is taken away by the paramedics, he forces Ben to admit
the truth.

Frank Dominic then makes his appearance, accompanied by his en-
tourage, announcing his official candidacy and introducing himself as a
descendant of the royal family of the Duke of Alburquerque, the Spanish
viceroy for whom the city was named. He communicates his grand plan
for the city, which impresses the people at first, but skepticism slowly
seeps in: the ranchers outside the city see nothing in the plan for them,
and the abiding issue of water rights is raised once again.

The boxing match is about to begin, and Ben wonders if he should
finally break his promise to Cynthia and tell Abrán the truth. He approaches Abrán in the ring, but Frank pushes him away. The match
begins, and Abrán faces his challenger, Bo Decker, a Las Vegas fighter.
By the sixth round Abrán's leg wound begins to bleed, and Ben demands
that Frank stop the fight. Frank refuses. Big money is riding on the game,
and it is clear that Frank has bet against his own fighter and is willing
to sacrifice him. Since Abrán is the hometown boy the crowd cheers him
on, even as he staggers on his feet, clearly wounded. Abrán's manager
begs Frank to stop the fight, but again he refuses to do so. Lucinda finally

makes her way into the auditorium and, seeing Abrán's condition, calls out to him. Frank orders her to be taken away, but Ben finally gathers the courage to defy him. Just then Lucinda tells Abrán the truth, which releases Abrán from his obligation to Frank. Nevertheless, after father and son acknowledge each other, Abrán musters up the energy to reenter the match. The revelation of his parentage has freed him from his doubts; to Frank's dismay, he wins the match.

The final chapter finds Abrán in the hospital, recuperating from his wounds. Frank's schemes have backfired, Joe is starting to get his life in order, and Lucinda and Abrán plan their future together. Ben visits Abrán's hospital room, and his closing thoughts as a character appear to be those of Anaya. For now that Cynthia's story has been fully told and the characters are ready to end their tale, Ben muses, "I think I've found a way to end the novel I'm writing" (292).

CHARACTERIZATION

The fictional world created in *Alburquerque* is a continuation of the one begun in *Bless Me, Ultima*; some characters are carried over from the one novel to the next, in new settings and circumstances, with new characters added along the way. Ben Chávez, as noted, is Benjie from *Heart of Aztlán*, later referred to as "Tortuga" in the novel of the same name. He is older now, a college professor and an artist, a role assigned to him at the end of *Tortuga*, when he discovered that his purpose in life was to "sing" the story of his people. In *Alburquerque* he continues to tell that story, weaving it around Abrán González's search for identity and that of the other characters in a changing environment. Ben Chávez as a character is also a thinly veiled reflection of Anaya himself. Ben will appear in later novels, not as a main character, but as an observer of events, occasionally with references to actual writings or activities associated with Anaya. Cynthia is also a carryover from previous novels: she was Cindy in *Heart of Aztlán*, the *gabachita*, or Anglo girl, from the rich neighborhood who was first attracted to Benjie's brother Jason but was later impregnated by Benjie after being rejected by Jason. The follow-up to their tale is one of the secrets that Ben Chávez will now be forced to reveal.

Indeed, integrity and authenticity, both personal and collective, form a dilemma faced by most of the characters. The personal identity that Abrán González had held for so long is shattered by the revelation of his adoption, obliging him to seek his authenticity; but most of the characters had begun the process of reinventing their identities long before: Walter and Vera Johnson created a new identity for themselves in order to gain social acceptance; Joe Calabasa attempts to regain his Native-American identity in order to reenter the circle of his pueblo; Frank Dominic identifies himself with a Spanish lineage to obtain a useful social pedigree; and Ben Chávez struggles to find himself and his authenticity in his stories. A more genuine and straightforward character, Lucinda Córdova recalls female characters from previous Anaya novels: she is a healer and an intuitive dreamer who inspires men with her goodness and beauty. Lucinda and her family are a part of their surroundings: they share their family surname, Córdova, with the area in which they live, and her father has adopted the name of Oso as a result of his identification with the animal world. They are aware of their origins and in tune with their culture, which is the source of their strength.

In a departure from realism, Anaya introduces a fantastical element with several characters. The two homeboys, Juan and Al, begin as literary characters within the novel, protagonists from an epic poem that Ben is writing, and then come alive to interact with other characters in an example of fiction within fiction (both characters are in fact the protagonists of Anaya's 1985 mock-epic poem *The Adventures of Juan Chicaspatas*). Likewise, Coyote and Doña Loneliness are other fantastical figures inhabiting another level of reality.

Many of the characters in the novel are referred to as "coyotes," a word interchangeable with the Spanish *mestizos*, that extends beyond racial and/or ethnic intermarriage to the blending of cultural traditions and worldviews. Abrán, Joe, Cynthia, and Vera represent a New World complexity that Anaya considers the subject of his writing: "what I have written and what I am writing is a search for a unique person, a person that has not been written about very much in the literature of the United States. . . . [T]his New World person, essentially he is a mestizo, he is myself and that's what I've been exploring in my writing" (Jussawalla and Dasenbrock, *Interviews* 255).

THEMES

The rapid economic growth in recent decades of the U.S. Southwest, America's Sun Belt, and specifically of such urban centers as Albuquerque, New Mexico, has produced sociopolitical consequences that concern authors like Rudolfo Anaya who feel a cultural and spiritual bond with the area. Who will control this growth? Who will be the winners and losers in the process? What will happen with the natural environment and the traditional peoples of the region?

Alburquerque confronts these issues via a personal story of change, growth, and eventual victory of an individual character. Abrán González will ultimately achieve his quest by discovering not only his biological father's identity but his own self in the process. The knowledge of his identity, combined with the support of his community, will give him the strength to attain victory in the boxing ring and overcome his interior bouts with fear and anxiety. But not everyone in the novel is as concerned with authenticity. As discussed in the previous section, many labor to hide their true identities as they invent newer, more convenient ones. Secrets and lies affect not only Abrán but most of the other major characters. Cultural heritage or social backgrounds are added or dropped whenever suitable. *Alburquerque* argues precisely for the opposite: a genuine appreciation and respect for the past that would eliminate the need for this subterfuge. References are made throughout the novel to cultures and groups that have been undervalued and thus threatened by the arrival of new dominant economic forces (see "Alternative Reading" below) and by a new generation in danger of forgetting its cultural roots.

Two scenes in particular illustrate the latter point. Cynthia's diary excerpt in Chapter Eight portrays a defiant, cocky, younger generation of urbanized Hispanics confronting their elders. They quickly realize that, in fact, the earlier generation still has useful lessons to teach. In Chapter Sixteen, as Joe Calabasa assists in the communal preparation of the irrigation ditches with the other members of his tribe, he is reminded of the effect on his life of his separation from his roots. Leaving the clan pushed him out of the center to the lonely edges, the periphery, where one is in danger of losing one's "spirit." The young generation of university-trained Native-American attorneys have, in fact, done just that; their modern, pragmatic perspective will lead them to recommend that the tribe's water rights, its cultural legacy, be sold to Frank Dominic, disregarding centuries of custom and tradition.

But *Alburquerque* is also about the role and responsibility of the artist/ intellectual as memory, conscience, and healer. Cynthia's value as an artist lay not only in the fact that she could capture the essence of her ethnic heritage in her work, but also in that she was able to document a culture in danger of disappearing. Similarly, Ben Chávez must tell a story that has remained hidden for too long. His literary themes reflect

the condition of his city and his people, but he must now also blend the
political with the personal if he is to cure the wounds of those closest to
him. Only then will his stories truly "bring a healing" and a closure
(292).

ALTERNATIVE READING: A POSTCOLONIAL VIEW OF
ALBURQUERQUE

The emphasis that *Alburquerque* places on the consequences of the historic displacement of peoples and cultures in the U.S. Southwest lends
itself to an interpretation based on postcolonial criticism, an area of study
that has its roots in shifting world events in the 1950s and 1960s. A
heightened consciousness regarding European colonialism as a model of
political power began during this period of anticolonial struggles in Af-
rica and Indochina. Among the intellectual analyses that emerged to provide a context for the burgeoning wars of liberation, Frantz Fanon's *The
Wretched of the Earth*, published in 1961, had a significant impact. Fanon
saw the racist attitudes of the West as a type of scapegoating that rationalized the power of empire to maintain its dominant position. The
imperial powers, he argued, had created a hierarchical classification of
the world's peoples in which those of European heritage, given their so-
called superior culture, were assumed to be the born rulers of subjugated
peoples deemed primitive and uncivilized, thus justifying slavery and/
or colonial domination. The denigration of colonized peoples led to a
process of intellectual "erasure" in which the language, culture, religion,
and history of those outside of the European model—the "other"—were
dismissed or totally ignored. The colonized were removed from history.
Postcolonial studies therefore create a dialogue that questions the Eu-
rocentric value system and its consequent biases.

The effect of European domination in such settler colonies as the
United States is also the subject of postcolonial criticism. In the United
States the descendants of Europeans replicated colonial policies with the
native peoples of North America and the Hispanics of the Southwest,
often referred to as the "internal colonies" or "the colony within." The
geographic and economic displacement of these peoples as a result of
U.S. expansionist policies was accompanied by their cultural domination
in a society in which the educational and social institutions were reg-
ulated and controlled by the descendants of European Americans.
As a result, the Western (Euro-Anglo) culture was privileged and the

Native-American and Hispanic traditions were neglected or repressed. A postcolonial reading strategy focuses on these issues and asks such questions as the following: Does a work favor Euro-Anglo culture, or does it reject such colonial stereotypes? Are other voices outside of those of the dominant culture heard, or are they ignored? Given the importance that postcolonial criticism (and Anaya's fiction) assigns to history, a brief historical review of New Mexico is in order.

Spanish domination and colonization of the area of New Mexico began in 1598 (Santa Fe was founded in 1610). Despite the Spaniards' attempts to impose their rule and their culture on the indigenous population, Native-American resistance persisted. Although the Pueblo Indian revolt of 1680 caused many Spaniards to flee, by 1696 they had reconquered the area, thereafter recognizing the Pueblos' title to their ancestral lands. In the eighteenth century new towns were established, including Albuquerque, which was founded in 1706. In 1821 Spain relinquished its North American possessions. The area became a province of the newly independent nation of Mexico, which permitted the entrance of U.S. citizens.

These citizens began to appear in greater numbers, initiating a long history of culture clashes among the Anglos (Americans of unmixed European origin), the Hispanics (New Mexicans of Spanish/Mexican/Native-American ancestry), and the Native Americans. In 1841 the Texas republic attempted to seize New Mexico; in 1846, when President James K. Polk declared war on Mexico, General Stephen Watts Kearny and the Army of the West were sent to invade. Kearny proclaimed New Mexico part of the United States in 1846. Residents of the area became U.S. citizens when the United States defeated Mexico in 1848.

Prior to the twentieth century the area was considered a "foreign" land: the Spanish language, traditional cultures, and a reputation for lawlessness created the notion of New Mexico as an exotic "other." For sixty-two years New Mexico remained a territory; fears that a Spanish-speaking community might not adjust to a U.S.-type democracy, among other issues, precluded statehood. In 1898 English began to be taught in the public schools, and on January 6, 1912, New Mexico, the nation's oldest established society, was admitted to the Union as the forty-seventh state. In 1943 the atomic bomb was created in the secret city of Los Alamos, and in 1945 the first atomic bomb was exploded near Alamogordo, south of Santa Fe. Military and nuclear research installations have contributed to the state's economy, and in the late twentieth century tourism has also become a major industry attracting people to an area that attaches great significance to its unique and diverse cultural heritage. How much concern, however, has the area attached to the descendants of this heritage, whom many consider its victims? *Alburquerque* poses this question.

Anaya has referred to the contemporary dynamics of Southwest urbanization as a "new model of colonialism" (Jussawalla and Dasenbrock, *Interviews* 253). *Alburquerque* takes full advantage of every occasion to insert history into the narration, assuring that readers will not forget the old models of colonialism imposed in New Mexico. Often this is accomplished via the historical reflections of the characters themselves. Frank Dominic identifies with the political vision of Spanish explorers and conquistadors, a more "acceptable" Hispanic alternative than a Mexican identity given its European origins; Abrán's mother, Sara, reminds him of the land grants of the original families who were later displaced by the Anglos; Cynthia paints the urban "outcasts" who are the descendants of those who had established Albuquerque and Santa Fe; and Lucinda Córdova's father blends family history with New Mexican history when he contrasts the official, unrealized promises of protection by General Kearny's invading troops to the reality of unscrupulous Anglo land appropriation, a story described as a "history of loss" (173).

Despite attempts to keep language and culture alive, the colonial marginalization of peoples continues to the present day. The urban development plans of persons like Frank Dominic, for example, will keep the conquered peoples in subservient, menial positions in his tourism schemes; they will become the exotic "other" who perform sterile folkloric dances and empty ceremonies for tourists, far removed from their authentic spiritual rituals of the past. But *Alburquerque* radically expands the question of conquest and imperialism far beyond the borders of New Mexico and the U.S. Southwest. Joe Calabasa has his own experience of empire building during his time in Vietnam. There he experiences an epiphany, a moment of psychic liberation from the alien values imposed on him as a Native American and a U.S. soldier. In a telling scene he realizes that the Vietnamese enemy he had been sent to destroy was akin to his own Indian grandfather—another colonized, dispossessed person, another victim of colonial models of social arrangements. He refuses to kill the old Vietnamese man who has also suffered the abuses of colonialism and imperialist wars; he cannot because, "In his face I saw the face of my people" (51).

Zia Summer
(1995)

Zia Summer represents Rudolfo Anaya's first foray into the classic American genre of mystery/detective fiction (discussed in chapter 2 of this book) and the introduction of a new detective character into the body of North American letters, Sonny Baca. Detective fiction may seem an unusual departure for Anaya, whose writing is so identified with mythical and cultural themes, but *Zia Summer* is not a radical change of direction for Anaya at all: the novel examines the politics surrounding crucial ecological issues that directly affect Anaya's beloved New Mexico, reflecting his ongoing concerns for the preservation of and respect for the environment and traditional cultures. The novel stresses the importance of myth in the growth and development of the individual and the community, illustrating Anaya's distinctive cultural approach to a quintessential American genre.

HISTORICAL BACKGOUND

The stories in Rudolfo Anaya's novels are, of course, the products of his creative imagination, but whenever possible the author will allude to historical events in his portrayals of characters that permit him to explore themes relative to Chicano cultural experience. In *Zia Summer*, in addition to the background information Anaya usually provides on the

Native-American and Hispanic populations of the New Mexico area, he has furnished the leading character with a unique past that rationalizes Sonny Baca's personality and motives, specifically a flamboyant and renowned ancestor based on the historical figure Elfego Baca.

Born in 1865 in New Mexico, Elfego Baca was the celebrated sheriff of Socorro County, an area renowned for its silver mines and its lawlessness. Baca's fame is the stuff of legends. It is said that at age nineteen he held eighty Texas cowboys at bay for thirty-six hours with his quick draw and deadly aim; he was as famous as Billy the Kid but on the side of law and order as sheriff, marshall, district attorney, school superintendent, and mayor. Having taken a gun from the Mexican revolutionary Pancho Villa, the latter retaliated by offering a $30,000 reward for Baca, dead or alive (Baca escaped Villa's wrath and died at age eighty in 1945). The colorful Baca has become the theme of novels and plays and even of a Walt Disney movie in 1958 titled *Nine Lives of Elfego Baca*.

CHARACTERIZATION

Readers familiar with Rudolfo Anaya's fiction know that he is an author concerned with the change and growth of his protagonists, or main characters. From his earlier coming-of-age novel *Bless Me, Ultima* to his work that immediately preceded *Zia Summer, Alburquerque*, an Anaya protagonist must face a task or quest that will lead to the self-knowledge required to accomplish his or her purpose or destiny. Sonny Baca, the detective protagonist of *Zia Summer*, will meet a similar challenge. The novel will trace his professional maturation and development, which is inextricably linked to his personal and cultural identity.

Anaya offers the reader access to Sonny Baca's insights through the technique of indirect discourse, a technique that associates the third-person narrative viewpoint with a particular character. In other words, the main character does not voice his feelings and thoughts directly as would be the case in first-person narration; rather, the omniscient, or all-knowing, narrator speaks them for the protagonist, offering the reader a subjective and intimate view of the character's internal emotions and motivations. This, in turn, allows the reader to share the sensation of suspense with the protagonist as the book's events unfold. The reader thus identifies more directly with the lead character, understanding his actions and the workings of his inner mind, as well as seeing events and other characters from his perspective. In this case, we hear Sonny Baca's self-doubts, his recriminations, and his fears. The result is a protagonist that is often more developed, sympathetic, and complex.

Dreams are also a recurring motif in Anaya's fiction, and they play an important role in *Zia Summer* too, structuring the novel, providing a framework. Dreams are an insight into the protagonist's development, occasionally foreshadowing events that will effect the outcome of the plot. *Zia Summer* begins with one such dream, a nightmare in which a woman attempts to emasculate Sonny Baca by aiming a chain saw between his legs. The grim dream hints at events that will come full circle by the novel's end, when Sonny will indeed be at the mercy of ominous and life-threatening females.

The motivation for Sonny's professional aspirations comes from his identification with his great-grandfather (*Bisabuelo* in Spanish; Spanish words are interspersed occasionally throughout the novel, providing local color and authenticity to the dialogue of the Chicano characters), who was a famous New Mexican private detective and lawman. Elfego Baca, an imposing and extravagant figure dressed in a cape, is a hero to the local Chicanos, who are well aware of the historic escapades of this Robin Hood–type lawman who stood up to abusive Anglos. Elfego Baca's fame nevertheless suffered the same fate as other Hispanic historical figures; his reputation was overshadowed by Anglo figures "because history wasn't fair" (3).

Sonny was in fact named after his famous ancestor, but his English-speaking schoolteachers were unable to pronounce "Elfego" and began calling him Sonny instead, even writing that name on his report card. Despite his father's objections, the name stuck. Sonny's mother decided that the name suited him. Sonny is a name that recalls the powerful New Mexican sun. Though Sonny Baca is a college-trained, thoroughly modern, urban Chicano, he identifies with his ancestors and with other such heroes. His decision to enter the detective profession was based on this identification and on such fantasies as one might expect of a novelist of the detective genre: "His mind was always active, always creating stories, and he made himself the hero of each story" (3).

After an unsatisfying teaching experience, Sonny learned his new profession from Manuel Lopez, with whom he solved some minor cases, including one that gained him notoriety. He and Manuel had solved the kidnapping case of the wife of a prominent car dealer who was hidden in the Chihuahua Mountains of Mexico. After spiriting her back across the border at Juárez, the local media made the pair famous. The job suits his personality: Sonny prizes his freedom, a good challenge, and adventure, even taking up rodeoing on weekends to fit his image as a "no-bullshit vaquero" (7).

Handsome, thirty years old, and unmarried, his sense of adventure extends to women as well. Attractive to women and divorced from his first wife, Sonny has played the field but is now involved with a woman with whom he fears he may be falling in love. Rita Lopez runs her own restaurant, Rita's Cocina, and will play an increasingly important role in his life.

As in the case of many other Anaya fictional characters, Sonny Baca has deep family roots in New Mexico and a diverse ethnic heritage: Spanish, Arabic, and possibly Jewish (via the Spanish explorers) ancestry combine with French Canadian, German, Navajo, and Apache in "a grand mestizo mixture": "All bloods ran as one in the coyotes of Nuevo Mexico" (5).

A dramatic crime will put Sonny Baca to the test in many ways; his skills as a detective and his personal identity will be challenged when he attempts to solve the bizarre murder of his cousin, Gloria Dominic. Similar to other works of this type, the initial puzzle he must unravel will turn out to be part of a larger one, with multiple and intricate pieces that will lead to a greater crime of much more serious consequence and wider repercussions. The victim is a character readers of Anaya's other novels have met before; she is mentioned in his previous novel, *Alburquerque*, as the wife of the ambitious and ruthless mayoral candidate Frank Dominic. (Other characters from Anaya's previous novel are repeated here as well, notably, Gloria's Japanese lover, the businessman Akira Morino, and Ben Chávez, a character that is clearly self-referential, an allusion to Rudolfo Anaya himself. In *Zia Summer* Chávez plays a minor role, as opposed to his status in *Alburquerque* as a major player. Ben Chávez is a writer and a university professor who had taught Sonny Baca a course in creative writing; according to Chávez, "A writer is like a good detective, always looking for motives" [86].)

Gloria had been important in Sonny's life, as she was his partner in his initial sexual experience and someone he had cared for deeply. Her death is particularly gruesome: her body had been drained of its blood, and around her navel had been scratched the four radiating lines of the Zia sun sign, the sacred sign of the Pueblo Indians of New Mexico and the symbol used on the state flag. Despite Frank's objections and those of the local police—both of whom want Sonny to keep out of the case—he will investigate out of a sense of family responsibility; his aunt, Tía Delfina, has asked him to find her daughter's murderer, and Sonny feels an obligation to Gloria herself, whose spirit begs him to avenge her death. He senses something cold enveloping him as he observes her life-less body—*susto*, or fright, Rita will call it, a restless soul haunting the living.

Sonny will have little official help in his investigation due to a tense relationship with the police chief, Sam Garcia. Some valuable assistance will come from his friend in the city's forensic lab, Howard Powdrell, but Sonny's more significant inspiration will come from an unlikely source, his old neighbor Don Eliseo. A repeated motif in Anaya's novels is that of the older teacher, the traditional role of the elder, who imparts knowledge of nature and ancient culture to the young. Sonny Baca is open to these teachings and, despite his young age, enjoys being in the company of older people like Don Eliseo and his friends. These charac-ters instruct Sonny in the old ways but are also helpful in his investi-gation; Don Eliseo will play a crucial role in solving the crime, warning him to beware of false clues and ultimately saving Sonny's life. In mo-ments of doubt or of danger, Sonny's memory resorts to the memory of his great-grandfather, to the lessons he learned from his late mentor in detection, Manuel Lopez, and to the wise guidance of his spiritual men-tor, Don Eliseo.

Among the more intriguing characters that Anaya will introduce in this novel and repeat in future works is the evil Raven, a *brujo* (shaman/ sorcerer), cult leader, and eco-terrorist who has the power to change into animal forms at will. Raven is a man of multiple identities, at once a sophisticated, charismatic environmental activist, able to attract the city's elite classes to his cause, and a ruthless, power-hungry cult leader who enslaves women and children and thinks nothing of destroying human life. Described in the novel as a man with a commitment, the "fervor of a religious fanatic, and the eyes of the prophets of the desert" (99), Raven is intelligent and articulate; his arguments concerning the environment are convincing and logical. Raven's antinuclear group has focused atten-tion on the Waste Isolation Pilot Plant (WIPP), a nuclear waste dump near Carlsbad, where dangerous high-level plutonium will be stored. The first delivery of radioactive wastes to the facility is scheduled for June 21, the first day of summer, and Raven plans to prevent the deliv-ery. Indeed, Sonny agrees that the environment is threatened by the con-tamination produced in the state by the nuclear and military industries; Sonny's father was a victim of such contamination, as Raven often re-minds him. What Sonny opposes is Raven's method for dealing with the problem; exploding a truck carrying nuclear waste material will cause the senseless destruction of lives and of nature that cannot be justified by good intentions.

Raven is assisted in his endeavors by a talent he has acquired in his role as brujo: he can assume at will the animal form corresponding to his name (one of Raven's alternate names is "Anthony Pájaro" or Bird). Appearing as a raven or crow, Raven can be in several places at once, facilitating his evil deeds. The belief in a *nagual* or *nahaul* (an animal double) dates from pre-Columbian (prior to the arrival of Christopher Columbus) times and still exists in Mexican oral traditions. The idea is not new to Anaya novels; it appeared in his first work, *Bless Me, Ultima*, where the character of Ultima has a double in the form of an owl. A nagual is not necessarily an evil attribute: it can be of assistance to a shaman, or a trained healer, who knows how to benefit from the powers of the animal spirit (see discussion of shamanism in chapter 8 in this book). With the help of a *curandera* (healer), Sonny must learn how to use his potential powers for good and tap into the spirit of his own animal double, the coyote.

Female characters play a more active role in *Zia Summer* than in previous Anaya novels. Although they act as inspirations and romantic interests for the male protagonists in most of Anaya's works, in *Zia Summer* female characters like Rita are more directly involved in affecting the plot: women will be the victims, aggressors, and assistants in the resolution of the mystery. Fundamentally one-sided characters representing certain qualities (Rita as the intuitive, loving, loyal companion in tune with her culture; Tamara Dubronsky, the seductive, socialite temptress, "queen of the Zia Sun"; Lorenza Villa, the spiritual healer/curandera; Veronica Worthy, the slavish evil cult wife; and Gloria Dominic, the beautiful but abused female), they nevertheless play pivotal roles in the novel. Rita will accompany Sonny in his quest to prevent Raven from exploding the nuclear waste truck and be instrumental in saving his life.

Anaya's concern that the old ways of his New Mexican culture are in danger of vanishing as the younger generations disregard the teachings of the elders is underscored in the care and joy he exhibits in the creation of his older characters. (Indeed, the novel is dedicated "to the old people who walk on the Path of the Sun and who remind us that clarity of the soul is possible, even in these violent times.") Don Eliseo plays an important role in the novel: he is Sonny's spiritual guide, an inspiration in his moments of danger and a teacher in the ways of the past. He is presented as an amiable figure who appreciates nature, friendships, and good times. His two friends, Don Toto and Doña Concha, are colorful, ribald characters who provide touches of salty humor to the novel, as in the hilarious scene in which Sonny invites his octogenarian neighbors to watch a game of professional baseball (258–264). Don Toto is an eighty-year-old who chases women and is described as "the terror of the gray-haired bingo ladies," and Doña Concha is "the most independent Chicana in the North Valley" who has survived the wives of Don Toto and Don Eliseo and now has both of them to herself (70–71). They are as resilient as nature itself. The novel in fact opens with the unsuccessful attempt to cut down Don Eliseo's ancient cottonwood tree, an alamo condemned by the city but one that has been witness to a hundred years of history. The tree, tough and durable like Don Eliseo and the other "ancestors of the valley" (60), with roots stretching to the past, will survive and surprise everyone at the end when it demonstrates miraculous signs of renewed life.

PLOT DEVELOPMENT

In many ways *Zia Summer* follows the generic conventions of the classic detection novel: the story opens with the dramatic description of a bizarre and puzzling crime; it follows a specific detective's investigation through scenes in which he confronts a number of intriguing characters and uncovers information, some of which is useful and some of which is not (the "false clues" that Don Eliseo warns Sonny against); and it closes with a solution to and a plausible explanation for the crime. But the description of the physical and social environment, which is crucial to the story, provides Anaya with the opportunity to dramatize the spiritual and cultural themes for which he is noted: respect for the environment and the American-Hispanic traditions and historical experiences of the Southwest.

The narrative plot of *Zia Summer* revolves around the criminal scheme devised by Raven, a fact the reader will discover along with the protagonist halfway through the novel. The initial murder case of Gloria Dominic is only one step along the way of Raven's mission to explode a truck carrying high-level radioactive waste to "scare the world to its senses" (322) and, in the ensuing chaos, to assume power and control. Before Sonny comes to that realization there will be several suspects: a cult of females that had taken over Gloria's life in the guise of curing her; Gloria's husband, an ambitious man with other lovers and a $2 million insurance policy on his wife; Gloria's Japanese lover and the father of her unborn child; and Gloria's drug-dealing brother, Turco Dominguez.

The twists and turns of the narration of Sonny's investigation of Gloria's murder will pause for his many reflections on matters not always related to the case. Anaya takes advantage of every opportunity to insert Chicano history and culture into his novel, working it into the lives of the characters and Sonny's frequent musings. Chapter Seven, for example, introduces a discussion of New Mexican history and culture as it develops the characters of Don Eliseo and his friends; background information on characters often provides the occasion for illuminating information on New Mexican historical experiences. Likewise, Sonny's reflections on the case are frequently combined with his ideas regarding social and economic development plans that disregard the area's unique cultural qualities.

Sonny will be misled by clues set to distract him throughout the novel, something Don Eliseo warns him to avoid. An example is his investigation of cattle mutilations in a village outside the city, a mishap that nearly costs him his life. Sonny had heard of cattle mutilations of a strange nature that appear to have a link to Gloria's death: the animals' genitals are removed, and their blood is drained. When Sonny tries to investigate the village, people threaten him; they are wary of strangers and fearful. A mention of his ancestor gains Sonny their trust, however, and José Escobar, the owner of one of the slain animals, allows him to view the animal. The cow is surrounded by a circle of stones and black feathers, Raven's calling card. But Sonny soon realizes that the dead animal is a trap. Hearing Don Eliseo's warning voice in his mind, he is saved from a sniper's bullet by Escobar.

Sonny's mistakes continue. A visit to Raven's house, where he meets Raven's half-starved wives and children, is followed by a vicious attack on him by the FBI; Raven is *their* business, not Sonny's, they warn, and he is in their way. Sonny suddenly realizes that the case he is working on is part of a much larger issue that has been eluding him from the start. This scene in Chapter Fifteen is followed by Sonny's meditation on his errors and an illuminating vision. How could he have gone to Raven's house without doing his homework? How could he ignore Raven's plans that could so easily have been discovered in the local newspapers? Pausing to reflect on all that has happened, Sonny experiences an epiphany with nature. He senses a den of coyotes nearby and, closing his eyes, begins to blend images of Raven with Manuel Lopez and his great-grandfather, Elfego Baca. He sees in his vision the women at Raven's compound drawing around him, trying to hang him and carve his navel. Rita then appears to save him as Gloria's ghost taunts him for revenge. Like the opening dream in Chapter One, this too is a prophetic, warning vision. When Sonny awakens his focus is clear: Gloria's murder and Raven's plans are in fact one and the same case.

Sonny's insecurities with the case have affected him physically and emotionally—the image of Gloria appears to him in his intimate moments with Rita, preventing him from making love. He promises her that he will visit a curandera, Lorenza Villa, to help rid him of Gloria's haunting spirit. It is Lorenza who informs Sonny of his affiliation with the animal spirit of the coyotes: "When the animal spirit appears, it means they come to help. . . . It implies danger" (194). He will eventually require a cleansing ceremony to put Gloria's spirit to rest, but Lorenza also warns him of another animal energy being used against him: "You are being cut into, drained, and only because you have your own strength within you are you able to keep going. . . . [Y]ou are a brujo within, a powerful but kind shaman, but one without training" (195–196). An angry crow, a bird that has followed Sonny on many occasions, watches nearby.

In Chapter Nineteen Sonny visits Tamara to seek her help in obtaining a meeting with Akira Morino. She tempts him with a promise of psychic sex that can reveal past lives and Sonny's powerful unseen nature. The Zia sun symbol, which is becoming ubiquitous in all types of settings, permeates Tamara's home as well, including her bedroom, which is structured around its radiating lines. Tamara's strong attraction for Sonny is diminished by Don Eliseo's inner warning to stay away.

Shortly after Sonny has a chance run-in with Raven's followers, which affords him the opportunity to meet the local sheriff, an admirer of Sonny's famous ancestor, and the sheriff's infamous prisoner, Raven. Their chance meeting finally reveals the truth: Raven is Anthony Pájaro, the sophisticated environmentalist Sonny had met earlier at an opera fund-raiser and Tamara's lover. Raven denies any involvement with Gloria's murder but rationalizes antinuclear terrorist actions as a means of shocking the world to its senses: "on the day the sun stands still, I'll go down in history as the man who saved the Earth!" (220).

The day of the summer solstice is, of course, the day of the truck shipment to the WIPP storage site. Nowhere closer to solving Gloria's murder, Sonny resolves to see her brother, Turco, a ruthless drug lord who is in trouble with the Mexican drug mafia. Turco insults the memory of his sister by claiming that she never came through with the money he needed. Returning to Rita's home after the meeting with Turco, Sonny discovers a gruesome warning nailed to her porch beams: the bleeding testicles of a goat. Will Sonny be the next victim?

In Chapter Twenty-Five Sonny finally obtains a meeting with Gloria's lover, Akira Morino. The chapter begins with more of Sonny's reflections: homeless men on the street recall the economic changes in Albuquerque that are creating a marginalized class of people. His musings continue in Morino's office, which is decorated with dragons, prompting Sonny to note the parallels between ancient Aztec and oriental mythologies (a theme developed by Rudolfo Anaya in his travel journal, *A Chicano in China*). Morino confirms the fact that he was indeed Gloria's lover and the father of her unborn baby. He had given her the money she requested but not for her brother; Gloria planned to leave Frank Dominic and have the baby elsewhere. Morino had gone to see her the night she was murdered to discuss her fear of her group's control over her, but when he arrived she was already dead. As Sonny drives home from the meeting he senses that the case is about to break loose; at that moment so do the highly anticipated June rains.

Sonny hurries to be with Rita, suddenly feeling better about himself; nature has effected a healing process (282). But their intimacy is interrupted by an unexpected visit by Don Eliseo and his cohorts: the old people have located the castrated goat at the home of witches who plan to sacrifice it for the summer solstice. A reluctant Sonny tumbles out of bed to follow their important lead. Don Eliseo leaves Sonny alone at the site and returns for Rita. Sonny dozes off but, sensing danger seconds before he is attacked, he awakens to find himself hanging by the arms from a ceiling rafter, "like a sheep ready for slaughter" (294), surrounded by evidence linking the house owner to Gloria's murder. His attackers enter and are revealed to be Raven's wives; the main wife, Veronica, had been one of the women in Gloria's group. When Gloria attempted to leave them she was murdered and sacrificed, as, Veronica claims, he too will be at sunrise. She carves a Zia symbol on his stomach, marking him for death, and leaves a helpless Sonny, who can do nothing more than call on the spirit of his ancestor for help, a call that is answered by Rita and Don Eliseo. Sonny now understands why Gloria was murdered and by whom. The missing money added to the motive: Raven needed Gloria's money to finance his eco-terrorist scheme.

The final chapters have Sonny matching wits with Raven to prevent his deadly plan. Knowing the import of symbolism to Raven's philosophy, Sonny correctly guesses that the explosion attempt will be made at the Arroyo del Sol (Sun) Bridge. With his great-grandfather's pistol, and with Rita and José Escobar at his side, Sonny sets out to confront Raven. The two finally meet in a turbulent scene that thwarts Raven's plan. Rita shoots at Raven, preventing him from harming Sonny, and the struggle between the two men sends Raven falling into the raging waters of the flooded ravine. The gold Zia medallion Raven wore around his neck is now clutched in Sonny's hand.

Sonny Baca is not quite finished with his task, however; one last piece of the puzzle must be set in place. A visit to Tamara's house will clarify his doubts. Tamara is unconcerned with Raven's supposed death; his spirit will return, she says. As for Gloria, Tamara, "the Zia Sun queen," was the real leader of the group of women who had tried to heal Gloria of the wounds of her past, but Gloria's attempts to leave the group could not be tolerated. While she herself may not have killed Gloria personally, Tamara knows where Gloria's sacrificed blood is hidden. As the police arrive at her home to question her, Tamara's eyes rest on a vase on her patio. Howard Powdrell, Sonny's friend in forensics, confirms Sonny's suspicions: the vase contains Gloria's blood blended with earth. Placing the vase at the head of Gloria's grave, Sonny completes his final family obligation to Gloria and the close of his case. Anaya leaves some threads untied at the end of *Zia Summer*, however (for instance, Raven's location, Tamara's guilt), threads that will be taken up again in the sequel to this novel, *Rio Grande Fall*.

THEMES

Evil as a pervasive force is an important theme to the novel. Sonny Baca must find his cousin's murderer and along the way he will confront many evils that must be vanquished, notably, the potential destruction of the environment by a power-hungry brujo. How does he acquire the skills to meet these challenges? The novel suggests in several ways that the answer lies in Sonny's need to get in touch with his true self and his culture. If Sonny remains open to the process, he will receive guidance along the way from his ancestors (Elfego Baca), his elders (Don Eliseo), the intuition of women (Rita and Lorenza), and nature itself (his coyote double). A man of potential spiritual power, Sonny must learn how to dominate that power for good; others, like Raven, have learned to tap spiritual powers for negative aims. A knowledge of cultural background helps the reader of Anaya's novels, but like knowledge of the Spanish language, it is not a prerequisite to appreciating his works. Anaya guides his readers carefully and tactfully; we too learn along the way.

The significance of the Zia sun symbol, repeated throughout the work, is one example of Anaya the author as teacher. For those who have not seen the symbol on the flag of New Mexico, the novel explains that the figure is composed of a circle from which four points, of varying length, radiate. The number four is significant as it is the number most relevant to the cycles of life. The Earth has four directions; the year, four seasons; the day is divided into sunrise, noon, evening, and night; human life consists of childhood, youth, maturity, and old age. All these things are bound together in an endless circle of life and love.

The sun symbol, which originated with the Indians of the Zia Pueblo in ancient times, also represents a tribal philosophy regarding the basic harmony of the universe and the sacred obligation to develop a pure spirit, a clear mind, a strong body, and a dedication to the well-being of the people. This powerful symbol has been defiled and desecrated in the novel, however, as have so many of the positive elements of traditional cultures. "The Zia sun is sacred. . . . [A] living reality worth fighting for" (107), yet here it has become "a symbol of murderers" (158). The novel criticizes not only the appropriation of the symbol for Raven's nefarious purposes but also the commercial use of the symbol that has devitalized it of its original meaning and power and, by extension, the depleting effect of the commercialization of folklore and culture for the purposes of industry and tourism. A genuine return to the positive elements of traditional culture is Don Eliseo's message to Sonny (181–185) when he shares with the younger man the ideas regarding the sun as giver of life and the need to discover one's spiritual path. (Many of these ideas are more fully elaborated in Anaya's philosophical novel *Jalamanta*; see chapter 9 herein.) *Zia Summer* extends the obligation of passing on cultural traditions from the older generation to the next and the idea that younger people still have much to learn from their elders.

Much of the religious symbolism expressed in Don Eliseo's teachings and in the spiritual practices of the characters is a reflection of the phenomenon referred to as "religious syncretism," which characterizes religious practices in many parts of the Americas. Religious syncretism is what results from the combination, merging, and/or reconciliation of differing belief systems. In the Americas it emerged from the introduction and, frequently, the imposition of European religions first on the indigenous peoples and later on African slaves. Their original beliefs merged with those of the Christian religion to form a syncretized New World spirituality. Examples of religious syncretism can be found in the novel in Don Eliseo's prayers to both the Indian kachinas and the Christian *santos*, or saints, and in the equating of Tata Dios (God) with Grandfather Sun, the giver of life: "The old man saw the Cristo in the sun, he saw the kachinas of the pueblos and the santos of the church" (182). But syncretic rituals are practiced by the younger generation as well. For example, the Catholic Rita also engages in ceremonies "to pray for the sun's return" (327).

Religious syncretism resulted from the colonial history of the Americas, and, as Anaya insists on reminding his readers, conquest and colonization comprise the historical foundation of New Mexican reality. One of the most devastating effects of colonialism on the culture of the vanquished is the negation of their history. Sonny's reliance on the memory of his great-grandfather therefore goes beyond his personal needs: Chicano heroes of the past must be rescued from history in order for their memory to inspire the young. Colonization by the Anglos (English-speaking Americans of European ancestry) denigrated the history of the peoples they defeated. Sonny's conversations with the Japanese entrepreneur Morino affirm Anaya's idea of New Mexico as a "colony within" (see the "Alternative Reading" of *Alburquerque* in the previous chapter). When Morino compares New Mexico to Japan, saying that it is insular, having been a nation unto itself for so long, Sonny is quick to note a distinction: New Mexico is "a colonized nation . . . there's a difference" (270).

Ecological issues (discussed in the next section of this chapter) are also an important theme of the novel. Raven's plans may be outrageous, but his motives are based on problems that are real and critical. The natural world is being destroyed by a lack of sensitivity; mankind has lost touch with the environment and seeks only to exploit and control it. Raven's criminal plan has its roots in another form of criminal behavior: the destruction of the planet's resources for profit and gain. While the novel does not sympathize with Raven and his dangerous cult (they too have manipulated the Zia sun symbol for their own deadly purposes), it leaves little doubt that empathy does exist for the need to deal with the ecological problems Raven claims he will eliminate.

ALTERNATIVE READING: AN ENVIRONMENTALIST
PERSPECTIVE ON *ZIA SUMMER*

Readers of Anaya's writings are familiar with his deep respect and reverence for the natural world. Anaya has expressed on numerous occasions his intense identification with nature, which began in his youth, and the epiphany or illumination he experiences in his contemplation and contact with the natural world (see chapters 1 and 2 in this book). Rudolfo Anaya has a particular attachment to the land of his ancestors, New Mexico, the area in which he has spent the major part of his life and which is also the setting of most of his writings.

The U.S. Southwest is famous for its spectacular vistas and monumental landscapes; its deserts and mountains have inspired film directors, painters, sculptors, and literary artists for decades. The mystical emotions the area arouses, and its vast isolated expanses, have also attracted spiritual groups of many types to the area, seekers of truth and wisdom, especially in recent years. An area left underdeveloped for a long period after it became a state of the Union in 1912, New Mexico has undergone rapid growth and economic development in recent decades, particularly in the areas of Santa Fe and Albuquerque, as a result of tourism and the infusion of industries related to military and nuclear research. It should be recalled that the Los Alamos Scientific Laboratory in New Mexico, established in 1943, was the site of the development of the world's first atomic bomb, and such high-technology military facilities as the Sandia Laboratories and the Air Force Special Weapons Center are also located in the area. Many believe that a reliance on this type of technology ignores its deleterious effects on the Earth; environmentalists fear that humanity no longer functions in harmony with the planet, which must be protected from human greed.

Zia Summer asserts this environmentalist message in many and diverse ways. From a spiritual perspective, in tune with the Native-American reverence for the Earth, the novel emphasizes the idea of the need to be in harmony with the natural world. The Zia sun symbol is a reminder of that harmony and the balance with nature that is a sacred obligation of mankind. New Mexico is a special holy place, according to Don Eliseo, that attracts the good and the bad: "what attracts the angel attracts the diablo" (326). The evil he refers to is not only Raven and his cult; it is also the greed that gives rise to the creation of pollution that poisons the environment for profit. Sonny does not agree with Raven's methods for saving the Earth, but he concurs with Raven's analysis of the problem: "They've been storing high-level shit in this state for forty-five years. . . . The DOE [Department of Energy] and the Defense Department have stockpiled nukes in the Manzano Mountains. All that stuff they're storing and dismantling is seeping into the water! At WIPP the barrels will be corroded by the salt! It's poisoning the earth!" (218). Sonny wants none of this in his land, the same that nurtured his ancestors. He recalls the lesson he had learned from Don Eliseo: "the Earth was alive. . . . Somewhere men and women had to come to their senses and stop producing what they could not control" (322).

The scarcity of economic opportunities for the original inhabitants of the land, however, pushes them toward a type of development that endangers their well-being as it simultaneously fosters environmental damage. The novel criticizes the fact that as the radioactive waste continues to pile up in such facilities as the Los Alamos and Sandia Labs, storage sites required to house the material are becoming a source of much-needed revenue for native peoples. "The storage of radioactive waste had become big business" (322). In its critique of a technology out of balance with the natural world and of economic development that ignores the true needs of current and future generations of New Mexicans, *Zia Summer* addresses important and timely environmental and social issues.

Rio Grande Fall
(1996)

Rio Grande Fall is Rudolfo Anaya's sequel to *Zia Summer* and the second of three novels featuring the Chicano detective Sonny Baca as protagonist (*Shaman Winter* is the third). In *Rio Grande Fall* Sonny will perfect his craft, though his impetuous nature continues to cause him problems that his innate intuition and spiritual powers will help resolve. Baca had begun to tap his spiritual potential in *Zia Summer*; but he will be forced to develop that asset further in this book in order to match wits with his rival and archenemy, Raven.

Social and political concerns invariably find their way into Anaya's novels: in *Zia Summer* the author addressed the important issue of environmental degradation in New Mexico due to toxic nuclear waste. *Rio Grande Fall* expands the political focus to hemispheric concerns. Sonny Baca will have to confront local, national, and international political corruption and drug smuggling in his struggle against evil. But in true Anaya fashion the struggle is not restricted to the physical world: combining contemporary and ancient, material and supernatural, evil here will be quelled only when grasped in its true and profound complexity. This is the challenge that leads Sonny Baca on voyages in and through time and space.

NARRATIVE STRATEGIES

Rio Grande Fall continues a story started in *Zia Summer*, but it is a complete novel in and of itself. Nevertheless, a sequel can be better appreciated if the reader is provided with background information; thus the first five chapters provide a summary of events in *Zia Summer* and begin to unravel several threads left deliberately loose at the close of that prequel. The reader had never been told, for example, if Raven, the antagonist (the opposing figure to the hero or protagonist), survived his struggle with Sonny and his subsequent fall into a ravine. Tamara Dubronsky, Raven's lover and the Zia queen of his sun cult, had been taken away for questioning by the police, but the reader never discovered if she had been charged with a crime. Veronica Worthy, one of Raven's wives and followers, was arrested for Gloria's murder, but the reader is left unaware if she had implicated anyone else in the crime. Finally, Sonny remained tormented by Gloria's spirit at the end of *Zia Summer*, a condition that his girlfriend, Rita Lopez, had urged him to resolve by being treated by a *curandera*, or folk healer.

The early chapters of *Rio Grande Fall* therefore respond to the first novel's unresolved issues. But at the same time the reader gradually becomes aware that the current novel will pursue Anaya's enigmatic narrative strategy employed in the first—that is, just as a sequel to *Zia Summer* must unravel threads left untied there, a sequel to *Rio Grande Fall* will have to attend to this novel's loose threads. For the author has organized his novel in such a manner as to assure that certain issues remain pending for yet another sequel to resolve. Since *Rio Grande Fall* is followed by *Shaman Winter* in this trilogy, it should come as no surprise to the reader that Raven will again thwart all of Sonny's attempts to destroy him and will remain at large to cross the detective's path in the future.

As noted in the discussions of previous novels by Anaya in this book, the author pauses frequently in his narration for particulars concerning local cultural and historical experience, adding to the novels' interest. While maintaining unity and coherence of the story line, Anaya inserts material that expands the scope of the narrative, occasionally detouring to relate detailed accounts of local customs or engaging descriptions of the characters' peculiarities. The reader is immersed in the autumnal grandeur of a New Mexican landscape and the taste and smells of roasting chile peppers, for example.

In this book the opening pages of Chapter Twenty-Five demonstrate Anaya's digressions into historical background material. As Sonny awaits the arrival of the ex-CIA operative William Stone, he observes the old section of the city and reflects on the origins of "la villa de Alburquerque" and the role of the Hispanic population in the development of the area. Anaya wishes to assure that the readers of his works absorb information regarding the people and culture of New Mexico as they become absorbed in the exploits of his charming detective. In most cases these musings by the characters or explanations by the omniscient narrator are welcome illuminations; they feed the reader's hunger for the engaging details that express the unique local flavor and distinctive nature of New Mexican culture. As in other Anaya works, local flavor and color is also provided by the use of Spanish words and expressions, usually explained in the text for the non-Spanish speaker either with an English translation or by the context in which the word is used. Again, while an understanding of Spanish enhances the appreciation of the novel, it is not essential.

HISTORICAL BACKGROUND

Rio Grande Fall is a contemporary story of crime and corruption in present-day Albuquerque, but the background and motives for the crimes are inextricably linked to historical events in Mexico, in Central and South America, and in U.S. policies in Latin America. Previous Anaya novels focused on the geographic area of New Mexico and the U.S. Southwest; for Sonny Baca to solve the crimes of murder and drug trafficking in *Rio Grande Fall*, however, he must venture beyond the borders of his home region to discover the source of the evil. A familiarity with the historical events mentioned in the novel adds to the reader's appreciation.

Drug trafficking and the corruption it occasions in societies—the major motive for the crimes Sonny must investigate—are linked in *Rio Grande Fall* to the long and occasionally tense relationship between the United States and Latin America in which, especially since the 1950s, the United States has not hesitated to use the Central Intelligence Agency (CIA) to intervene, directly or covertly, in the internal affairs of any Latin American nations thought to be left-leaning. The example mentioned in the novel as an initial phase of this intervention is the coup against Salvador Allende in Chile in the 1970s. Those responsible for the drug trafficking from Colombia, via Mexico, into the United States in *Rio Grande Fall* are former CIA agents whose careers had included creating and supporting the Contras, an antirevolutionary army intent on toppling the Sandinista Revolution in Nicaragua in the 1980s.

The facts in the novel surrounding John Gilroy and William Stone (the flying in of weapons to the Contras in Nicaragua in exchange for drugs) are corroborated by the findings that have subsequently been disclosed surrounding the scandal that has come to be known as the "Iran-Contra affair," in which profits from the secret and illegal sale of arms to Iran by high-ranking members of Ronald Reagan's administration were diverted to set up a covert network of support for the Nicaraguan right-wing guerrillas: "the Contras traded war supplies for drugs. Cocaine was channeled into this country with the blessings of some very important people in the government" (159). The novel updates such historical and political issues with the suggestion that the CIA currently cooperates with the Mexican army in its attacks against the Chiapas peasant movement in southern Mexico and its leader, Comandante Marcos, whom the CIA has branded a communist.

Rio Grande Fall establishes that the end of the Sandinista Revolution in Nicaragua did not stop the flow of illegal drugs into the United States; the enormous amounts of money to be gained from drug trafficking generated more greed and more corruption, leading to the present-day problems faced by cities like Albuquerque. Alliances formed by U.S. government officials in Nicaragua during the anti-Sandinista campaign were shifted to the drug cartels in Colombia and later Mexico, increasing U.S. drug flows and addicting a new generation. An even greater motive beyond money, however, is power. Under the pretext of battling communism some U.S. agents were actually more interested in gaining control over high government officials in Latin America. "When key government figures wouldn't deal with them, they created anarchy. Their plan was to step in and rule" (161).

Rio Grande Fall does not ignore local historical events, however. There is a reference in Chapter Seven to the famous Chicano journalist Rubén Salazar, whose reporting focused not only on international issues but also on the full range of urban problems facing Chicanos in Los Angeles. Salazar was killed under suspicious circumstances by the Los Angeles police while covering the Chicano Moratorium, an anti–Vietnam War demonstration in Los Angeles in 1970. Elfego Baca (1865–1945), the renowned New Mexican lawman that Anaya has made the great-grandfather of his protagonist, is recovered from history once again in yet another Anaya novel (for a discussion of Elfego Baca, see chapter 7 in this book).

CULTURAL CONTEXT

The Chicano protagonist of *Rio Grande Fall* and his family and friends live multicultural lives; a part of the modern, Anglo, scientific world, they retain significant elements of their Hispanic/Native-American heritage. Examples of this *mestizo*, or mixed, tradition can be seen in several places: in religious syncretism, in traditional healing practices, and in a belief in the supernatural powers of certain individuals referred to as *brujos/brujas* (loosely translated as sorcerers, shamans, or warlocks/witches).

Religious syncretism (discussed in chapter 7 in this book) is the result of an ongoing process that integrates traditional beliefs with new religious practices; it reflects a dynamic pattern of continuity and change. In the Americas, when the Europeans imposed their religions on the indigenous peoples, they merged their original beliefs with those of the Christian religion to form a syncretized, New World spirituality. The character Lorenza Villa, for example, is a curandera, or spiritual healer, in the Native-American tradition who also prays to the Catholic saints (3); Rita's multicultural farewell combines several traditions, "Ve con Dios, los santos, y tu nagual" (Go with God, the saints, and your animal double [125]); and Sonny wonders if his guardian angel is the Catholic St. Christopher or the spirit of the coyote, his *nagual*, or animal spirit, in the Amerindian tradition: "Two worlds so far apart, and yet both were worlds of the spirits" (316). In some cases, however, the native peoples and others forced to accept a foreign belief system resisted, going underground to avoid persecution. The maintenance of traditional beliefs is the result of this defiance by such people as the Pueblo Indians and the Jews, among others: "With the coming of the Anglo Americans, the Nuevo Mexicanos did the same. The ceremonies of the church remained in the open, but the deeper beliefs and folk remedies, the stories of the brujos, went underground" (118).

Ideas surrounding brujos are an important element of Anaya's fictional world; in *Rio Grande Fall* witchcraft and the supernatural are fundamental to the plot and characterization. New Mexico's cultural diversity has long been associated with such beliefs. As Don Eliseo says in the novel, "The Río Grande valley was a sacred place, full of ancient spirits. Full of knowledge" (25). Raven is a brujo and corresponds to the lore surrounding such beings, ideas often associated in many belief systems with shamans or religious healers. Among traditional peoples of the world, the shaman is a spiritual healer and keeper of tribal history; he or she is believed to possess the ability to serve as a bridge between the physical and the spiritual world. The word "shaman" comes from the Tungus language of eastern Siberia, the site, according to anthropologists and historians of religion, of the origins of shamanism. A distinguishing characteristic of shamanism is its focus on the trance state. After strenuous training and initiation, the shaman's soul is believed to leave the body and ascend to the heavens or descend to the underworld. Other techniques include lucid dreaming (dreams play a significant role in shamanic trance states) and what is referred to as "out-of-body experiences" or "altered states of consciousness." One of the more fascinating specialties of the shaman is "shamanic flight," a voyage beyond the physical body. While in a shamanic trance, he or she is able to communicate with and control spirits, retrieve souls, and make distinct changes in reality that can affect the physical world. These experiences are of the type shared by Sonny, Lorenza, and Raven in *Rio Grande Fall*.

Raven and Lorenza are not actually labeled shamans in the novel but instead are referred to as "brujo" and "bruja," equivalent Spanish terms that comprise sorcerer, warlock/witch, medicine person, and herbalist, and that emphasize the magical aspects of spiritual powers. One of the brujo's powers is that of inhabiting the animal spirit, or nagual (see chapter 7 in this book for a discussion of the nagual in Native-American cultures). References in Chapter Three to "the world of the nagual" and "Don Juan" (25) are allusions to the protagonist of Carlos Castaneda's well-known book *The Teachings of Don Juan: A Yaqui Way of Knowledge* (1968), which documents Castaneda's adventures in the world of shamanic lore in Arizona. The brujo is said to possess the ability to enter the animal world and tap into that source of strength; a brujo/bruja can also, however, assume the animal form of his or her nagual spirit. Brujos require a ritual defense to defeat their evil powers: Raven, therefore, is invincible in his circle, but he can be weakened by another brujo. Lorenza, the curandera, has mastered the power of the animal world and is a bruja that can strike at Raven's powers. Sonny Baca must learn to do the same.

PLOT DEVELOPMENT

In the first chapter of *Rio Grande Fall* Sonny Baca is experiencing a *limpieza*, a spiritual cleansing performed by the curandera Lorenza. The cleansing should rid Sonny of *susto*, a haunting by the spirit of Gloria Dominic, his cousin killed in a gruesome ritualized murder (from the plot of *Zia Summer*). During the cleansing Sonny has an unusual vision of a body falling from the sky, a vision that will turn out to be prophetic. It is the first week of October and the beginning of the annual Hot Air Balloon Fiesta of Albuquerque (note that although Anaya maintains the original spelling of the city's name [Alburquerque] throughout the novel, in this chapter the modern-day spelling will be retained for clarity), an important international tourist attraction. A fatal accident will mar the event, however: Veronica Worthy, the state's prime witness against Tamara Dubronsky in the Gloria Dominic murder trial, has been pushed from a balloon, her body impaled on a tree. Sonny is certain that Raven is the killer. An anonymous phone call had informed the police of this accident, where Raven has left his signature calling card (clues that confirm his presence): four black feathers on the body. Raven, the eco-terrorist whose scheme to blow up a truck carrying nuclear waste material was thwarted by Sonny in *Zia Summer*, has returned to extract his revenge on Sonny and to continue his plans to wreak havoc and destruction on the world. Sonny notices a narcotics detective at the scene of the crime; it is the first mention of a drug connection that will continue to evolve in later chapters (13).

Chapter Three tells the story of Lorenza's apprenticeship in Mexico and New Mexico to enter the world of the brujos. It is the first time Sonny hears of the power of the brujo to fly and to transform the human body into that of an animal. The remainder of Chapter Three and Chapters Four and Five summarize events from *Zia Summer* (see the discussion on plot in chapter 7 herein) for readers unfamiliar with Anaya's previous novel. Chapter Six returns to the existing crime of Veronica's murder and the problem it poses for the Balloon Fiesta; the event is losing money as balloonists are reluctant to fly with a murderer on the loose. The director of the fiesta is an acquaintance of Sonny, Madge Swenson, a woman with whom he shares a "lustful chemistry" and who has asked him to help cover up the accident in the press. Sonny has earned a reputation in the city for the crimes he has solved in the past, but he refuses to compromise his integrity.

Instead, Sonny does some research. Poring over the list of the registered balloonists, three names stand out: Mario Secco is a well-known international drug trafficker; John Gilroy is an ex-CIA agent who was known to have traded arms for drugs to sponsor the CIA-backed Contras against the Sandinista government in Nicaragua during the Reagan administration; and Alisandra Bustamante-Smith is a Colombian journalist whose husband was murdered by the Cali drug cartel in revenge for her exposure of their illegal operations in the country. The fiesta organizers have temporarily solved their problems without Sonny: paid false witnesses lie on the fiesta's behalf, claiming that Veronica was alone in the balloon. Sonny's intuition tells him that there were real witnesses to the accident, however, the same ones who had called in the anonymous tip to the police. He decides to search the woods surrounding the site of the fall and comes upon a group of homeless people. Sonny wins their confidence, and they confirm his suspicions: Veronica was indeed murdered by a man who struck her and pushed her out of the balloon, a man who fits Raven's description. But Raven now has a new distinguishing feature: one side of his face is badly scarred, the result of the injuries he suffered at the end of *Zia Summer* in his struggle with Sonny, giving Raven even greater motive for revenge.

Sonny and Raven will meet on several occasions throughout *Rio Grande Fall*. Their first encounter occurs in Chapter Eight. Raven and his followers ambush Sonny in his home, threatening his life, which is saved by his neighbor Don Eliseo, the old man who is Sonny's mentor in the traditional ways of his culture. Sonny and Raven, he says, are ancient rivals in a struggle that began in past lives between two powerful souls: "He can't kill you with a pistol. . . . That's why he wants the sign of the sun on the medal you carry" (77). Sonny had kept Raven's gold Zia medallion after their struggle, and Raven wants it back. A visit to Tamara repeats Don Eliseo's strange message: Sonny is an old soul who, like herself, has lived many lives; Raven, she says, "is not of this world" (87).

After the murder of a second balloonist, the Italian drug smuggler Mario Secco, the fiesta organizers hire Sonny to solve the mystery. Among the board members of the event is a heart surgeon, Jerry Stammer, who had poured millions of dollars into his research on human heart transplants with baboon hearts; his unusual research had ostracized him from the medical community and left him in need of funding. Sonny's intuition leads him to the conclusion that the murders go beyond the elimination of two people to something much more complicated and dangerous. He accepts the case on the condition that his payment for solving the murders be in the form of a house for the homeless family he has befriended.

Sonny's plan for catching Raven is risky. The fiesta must cancel all flights and announce that Sonny will fly a balloon, hoping that this will draw Raven out. Before the flight, however, Sonny visits Lorenza to absorb more of her lessons and to experience the lucid dreaming or trance state that leads him to his coyote spirit in the underworld, from which he draws his strength. There Sonny is finally freed of Gloria's haunting spirit, an experience he compares to flying. The following day, with Madge Swenson, he enters a hot air balloon, a special vehicle enforced with layers of steel sheets on the floor according to Sonny's specifications. Raven's decoy balloon appears, firing dummy shots at Sonny's balloon while Raven takes aim at them from the ground. Sonny's foresight has thwarted Raven for now. Nearby an FBI helicopter, carrying a top CIA official implicated in the Contra scandal, William Stone, observes the confrontation. Why is the CIA interested in Raven? Traces of cocaine are found in the woods where Raven had waited for Sonny's balloon. There is talk around the city of a huge shipment of drugs from Colombia, a delivery that can enter the country only with government protection. The Balloon Fiesta, Sonny realizes, is a cover for the shipment, and Raven is involved for one purpose: he needs the money to bankroll his cult. Veronica's and Mario's deaths are a distraction intended to "create confusion and in the melee, the shipment was dropped, cut, and distributed" (153).

A meeting with the Colombian journalist Alisandra Bustamante-Smith provides Sonny with more clues. Mario Secco was her brother; he was killed so that ex-CIA agent John Gilroy and Raven could divide the drug money between themselves, and William Stone is also involved. Alisandra's insurance against further harm to herself and her child is a faded photograph of a man she believes to be William standing next to a cartel drug lord in Colombia, a photograph she now bequeaths to Sonny, hoping it may result in revenge for her husband's death. A stakeout of Gilroy's home leads Sonny to follow him on a hurried and unexpected flight to Juárez, Mexico, where Sonny's impetuous nature brings him face-to-face with Raven. Now Raven has the advantage. He and John leave Sonny for dead in a warehouse in which they will leave a portion of the drugs to distract the authorities while the real shipment is sent to the United States in used UPS trucks. Sonny narrowly escapes death once again, thanks to the arrival of the Mexican cabdriver who had driven him from the airport. It appears that Raven cannot destroy Sonny in a conventional manner.

Despite official fiesta restrictions against flying balloons, John Gilroy, a big contributor to the fiesta, has been given permission to fly by Jerry Stammer. Madge, who has a history of drug use, denies any connection to the smuggling plans when Sonny confronts her with the information, but Sonny now has an even greater problem to solve. His girlfriend, Rita, and the young daughter of the homeless couple they have befriended, Cristina, have been kidnapped by Raven. Lorenza had seen the crime in a vision and feels she can identify the place where they are being held. With Lorenza at his side and the coyote powers he has developed, Sonny will track Raven via helicopter to a warehouse in an area of the city referred to as "Infierno" (Hell). But once again Sonny falls into Raven's ambush. Tear gas blinds him and Lorenza, and both are tied up and shoved into a black inflated balloon. The ropes keeping it moored to the ground are cut, causing the balloon to rise rapidly into the cold, deadly atmosphere. With much effort Lorenza manages to stop the burner from firing, and the two sway down to the ground.

Raven still holds Rita, however, and Sonny knows he must find her soon. Within his circle, Raven is invincible; Sonny must tap into his own power to beat Raven at his game. Turco Dominguez, Sonny's drug-dealing cousin, reluctantly offers him a lead: Madge Swenson and John Gilroy are lovers. But Sonny will not be able to obtain John's side of the story, for he discovers the former agent murdered in his hotel room, where Sonny is almost killed himself by Raven. Police Chief Garcia arrives in time to save Sonny's life, but Raven escapes his grasp. The evil brujo has flown away, leaping over the hotel balcony to safety.

The Balloon Fiesta has resumed, and an eager crowd returns to the sky. On a hunch Sonny asks if there have been any unusual UPS shipments. He is told that an inordinate number of propane tanks have arrived suddenly; one of them, he discovers, is carrying drugs. But the bust is suspiciously simple. A leery Sonny realizes that it is yet another of Raven's decoys, a false clue to distract him while the shipment was delivered. Sonny decides it is time to go directly to the source, William Stone. He entices William with Alisandra's photograph, but their meeting brings him no closer to Rita and the child. Raven has double-crossed the CIA official as well: he has taken the drugs, and William is searching for him too.

Sonny must enter the center of Raven's world to save Rita, and Lorenza will be his guide. Raven, she explains, is a brujo of the underworld, born to evil (295), a spirit of chaos and destruction who wants to rule "the new time born from the ages of the old" (298). Sonny and Lorenza head for Raven's mountain clearing, the secret place where he changes into his animal form. Sonny gradually enters his own coyote spirit as Lorenza's owl eyes begin to shine; she too has her nagual. In an ominous circle surrounded by the cries of black crows, Raven awaits Sonny's arrival. Sonny must attempt to propel Raven from his center of power; their struggle is as between two snarling animals, two equals. But Raven gains the advantage and is about to strike at Sonny with his blade when Lorenza shoots him, temporarily stopping him from doing harm and permitting Sonny to save Rita and Cristina. Sonny has faced the evil brujo and has prevailed: "His nagual spirit had entered the world of the brujo. Now he believed that perhaps both Don Eliseo and Lorenza were right. He, Sonny Baca, was also a brujo" (308).

Sonny has one last battle to face, however. The drugs are still being held somewhere in Albuquerque, and Madge confirms his hunch: Jerry Stammer had murdered John Gilroy, and the drugs are stored in his baboon labs. Jerry needs the funds for his research, but when Sonny arrives to confront him with the information he winds up strapped to an operating table, soon to become Jerry's and Madge's next victim. With Madge's assistance, Jerry jolts Sonny's body with a heart stimulator. The first shock does not kill him, but just as Jerry prepares for a second jolt Tamara Dubronsky, called to Sonny's side in a vision, enters the room and kills Stammer. She takes pity on Sonny's convulsive body and places a dagger to his throat, feeling that death is preferable to life in that condition. But she is stopped from ending his life by the sound of police sirens. Sonny's out-of-body experience in the final chapter saves him; his coyote spirits snatch him from the path of death, sending him back to the world of light.

CHARACTERIZATION

In *Rio Grande Fall* Anaya resurrects many of the characters from *Zia Summer*. Sonny Baca is again a Chicano charmer, the great-grandson of a legendary lawman and an amiable sleuth who fights evil in its myriad dimensions. He is attractive to women and knows how to appreciate them. Although cynical at times about the ways of the world, he is kind-hearted and helpful to those less fortunate than he. Though Sonny's university training exposed him to the modern, scientific worldview, he understands the valuable lessons to be learned from the old traditions of his culture. A combination of old-fashioned detective work and Sonny's mystical inner force will thwart the evil intentions of his dark enemy, Raven. Theirs is the classic struggle of good versus evil.

Raven and Rita are *Zia Summer* characters reintroduced in *Rio Grande Fall*. Rita is Sonny's ongoing love interest, a woman whom, he often repeats, he will eventually marry, but not quite yet. She grounds him to the earth, to tradition, to his cultural roots. But other women can be dangerous for Sonny. Madge Swenson, a seductive socialite, draws him into a dangerous trap that almost ends his life; and Tamara Dubronsky, a psychic who claims to know Sonny from their past lives, wishes to lure him into a relationship to trap him emotionally.

Lorenza Villa, briefly mentioned in *Zia Summer*, has a more active role in *Rio Grande Fall*, where she will occasionally serve as Sonny's spiritual sidekick and guide, assisting him in the struggle against Raven. Lorenza offers valuable advice in a task that requires mystical knowledge above and beyond the average variety of detective work. Don Eliseo, also a *Zia Summer* character, plays a similar inspirational role in *Rio Grande Fall*. Characters that are completely new to *Rio Grande Fall* have minor roles: John Gilroy, William Stone, Alisandra Bustamante-Smith, and Madge Swenson impel the plot but are not fully developed characters—they are steps on Sonny's path to Raven.

An interesting device that Rudolfo Anaya began to employ in *Alburquerque* and continues in *Zia Summer* and *Rio Grande Fall* is using the character of Ben Chávez, a writer, as a representation of the author himself. Ben played a significant role in *Alburquerque*; and in *Zia Summer* references to him are clearly allusions to Anaya. In *Rio Grande Fall* the trend continues. Ben Chávez is first seen taking notes at the site of Veronica Worthy's murder; he knows everyone in the city, and "sooner or later he would write them into his novels" (14). Chapter Ten describes "the burning of the Kookoóee" ceremony, the effigy of the bogeyman of Hispanic folktales, also referred to as "el Coco." Rudolfo Anaya and other Chicano artists did burn an effigy of "el Kookoóee" during the summer of 1990 at a public fiesta in Albuquerque, creating a communal event to expose the younger generations to the Chicano cultural traditions that he fears are in the process of disappearing. "Chávez brought el Coco to life, Sonny thought, like he brings his characters to life. The writer *was* a brujo" (94).

THEMES

The title of *Rio Grande Fall* is a pun, or a play on words: it describes the season of the year in which the crime occurs as well as the nature of the initial wrongdoing—Veronica Worthy's fatal plunge from a hot air balloon. But much of the rest of the novel is also associated with a fall of one sort or another: a decline into corruption, a falling short of social responsibility, a falling away of values.

The drug issue is a descent into greed and depravity that affects all sectors of society. The novel asks the questions: Who benefits? Who suffers? Although some of the answers are dealt with within a global context (see the "Historical Background" section above), the novel makes clear that the consequences of these crimes are suffered most directly by the immediate community. The fallout of drug trafficking on the black and Chicano barrios, for example, is addressed. Those responsible for eliminating the scourge—the local police, the FBI, the Drug Enforcement Agency, and the CIA—create more problems than they solve, and the city government of Albuquerque has clearly fallen short of its duties, ignoring the needs of its most vulnerable citizens. The homeless family that Sonny and Rita befriend are the forgotten members of the city, reduced to living in fear for their survival, pushed to the edges of society. The positive values that had held people together, that sustained and nurtured communities in the past, are falling away, eroding. A favorite theme of Anaya, the novel decries the loss that this represents for the young: in forgetting their culture, they undervalue their elders, their community, and themselves.

The struggle of good versus evil is a repeated theme in Anaya's fiction, often situated within the context of the ancient and cosmic cultures of the Americas. Raven is a lord of the underworld, a figure who has survived centuries, a force beyond the physical world. Lorenza explains these ancient beliefs to Sonny in Chapter Twenty-Seven—the Aztec notion of the "Fifth Sun" (discussed in chapter 9 in this book) in which negative powers, in existence since the beginning of time, have always attempted to create chaos and strife in the universe. "Evil was loose in the world, and the morality that described humanity had been sapped. At that moment, when an old era was dying, the people had to decide which way to turn" (300).

To counteract this evil Sonny must learn to fly like the brujos. His training in the ancient ways will come from a curandera, a more reliable source of healing in the novel than conventional, scientific medicine. Spiritual healing is another favorite Anaya theme, not unusual for an author from the U.S. Southwest, where many people continue to rely on a heritage of herbs, spiritual healing, and folk practices. Although in some remote communities of the region, folk medicine is still the only kind of treatment available, an increasing number of people choose to see a curandera or medicine person while simultaneously receiving conventional medical treatment. The character Lorenza Villa, for instance, has a nursing degree from the University of New Mexico but recognizes that the older Hispanos are not being well served: "They got their shots, got their operations, then went back home to doctor themselves with the remedies of the ancestors. In other words, the doctors weren't taking care of their spiritual health" (22). Folk medicine is not presented in the novel as simply a time-proven curative practice; within its cultural context, it is yet another affirmation of cultural identity.

ALTERNATIVE READING: A FEMINIST ANALYSIS OF *RIO GRANDE FALL*

The international women's movement of the late 1960s—which had as its aim the social, political, and economic equality of the sexes—inspired a new approach to writing and reading, feminist literary criticism, in which gender became a criterion for literary analysis. A common concern of feminist criticism is the impact of gender on writing and reading from a broad perspective that includes political, sociological, and economic factors. Through a feminist analysis women could begin to make important connections between literature (by women and men) and their lives, their experiences as females in patriarchal, or male-dominated, societies.

Initially feminist readings analyzed the stereotypical portrayals of women characters and the lack of a feminist literary heritage. Feminist readings of classic works that had traditionally been evaluated only by male critics led to revised interpretations of these works and a heightened sensitivity to sexism and the mistreatment of women. Given the important role assigned to Lorenza Villa, the curandera/bruja in *Rio Grande Fall*, a feminist anthropological reading of the character can help to illuminate Anaya's assessment of the role of women in Hispano/ Native-American culture.

Lorenza Villa plays a vital role in *Rio Grande Fall.* Thanks to her spiritual abilities and curative talents, Sonny Baca is able to tap his inner spiritual resources and confront his powerful enemy. Sonny is willing to accept her remedies because he trusts and respects Lorenza's knowledge; he realizes she has much to teach him. Lorenza represents the *mestiza* woman who is aware of her culture and the ways of her ancestors. A university-trained health professional, she has also labored hard to acquire her traditional skills, visiting old curanderas in northern New Mexico, the Hispano villages, and Indian pueblos, learning the world of herbs, massage, and the medical theories based on balance and harmony: "The healers there had been passing down remedies for centuries. Those women know how to care for the soul" (23). Women have passed on such knowledge from generation to generation.

Like many anthropologists, Lorenza became an ethnographer, one who studies the culture of a specific group of people. But her work is not that of the outsider looking in only to observe and describe; rather, Lorenza studies people in order to help cure them and to continue passing down their traditions. She has taken serious risks to pursue her goals, penetrating the male world of the brujos, "men who could fly" (24). Lorenza had to discover her own animal spirit, her nagual, as well as her female power, one that rivals that of the male brujo Raven in the novel. Traditional healing, becoming a curandera/bruja, became Lorenza's vehicle for self-empowerment.

The character of Lorenza corresponds to a history of traditional, spiritual healing that spans the world and in which women have played a significant role throughout history. Women have long been relegated the task of preserving cultural traditions from generation to generation, among them the ancient curative practices. Excluded from positions of power in conventional medicine for centuries, women have preserved effective nontraditional methods as a viable alternative. Their services have been undervalued and even dangerously maligned, however, as attested by the persecution of women throughout the centuries, often based on malicious charges of witchcraft. Victims of a misogynistic fear and hatred of powerful, strong women, they have been persecuted for practicing their traditional skills.

Through the character of Lorenza Villa, Rudolfo Anaya redeems the twentieth-century, multicultural female healer. Far from a figure to be feared or vilified, Lorenza's psychic abilities are used for good; her faculties are life affirming. Lorenza represents a vital female culture that contributes to the community; she is a resource, a trained specialist who uses her knowledge and talent to strengthen others and herself. Lor-

enza's spiritually oriented rituals respect all life energies: her nonhier-
archical connection to the animal world extends to her relationships with
both men and women. In Lorenza, Anaya has revindicated an object of
contempt and fear—a strong and powerful female in touch with her own
potential—and created a character who, like many Chicana feminists, is
making an attempt to revive the positive, empowering elements of her
culture as she struggles to become a full and equal member of her society.

9

Jalamanta: A Message from the Desert
(1996)

Jalamanta can be considered the culmination of Rudolfo Anaya's mythic vision, a vision begun in the early 1970s with his novel *Bless Me, Ultima* and continuing with *Heart of Aztlán* and *Tortuga*. *Jalamanta* is also, however, an outgrowth of two earlier novellas (short prose narratives described alternatively as "long short stories" or "short novels") written in the 1980s: *The Legend of La Llorona* (1984) and *Lord of the Dawn: The Legend of Quetzalcóatl* (1987). In both these works Anaya revisits mythic themes and characters that appear in his novels. A brief commentary on these novellas will assist our understanding of *Jalamanta*, a modern-day parable illustrating the message of personal and communal salvation through the power of love.

THE LEGEND OF LA LLORONA

The title of Anaya's novella reveals its intent: the reader soon discovers that the author has blended one legendary female figure—La Malinche, the Indian consort/translator of the sixteenth-century Spanish conquistador Hernán Cortés—with another, La Llorona, the wailing woman of Mexican-American folklore. In most versions of the folk legend La Llorona, as a result of a betrayal, killed her children in revenge, and her spirit is forced to wander near the banks of rivers, moaning and searching for her lost progeny. "Be good or La Llorona will get you" is a warning heard by many Hispanic children who grow up to fear sounds in the night that may herald the approach of the woman who has violently transgressed the role of mother. Likewise, the historical "Malintzin" (the original indigenous name of Malinche) has been reviled by Mexicans for centuries. She became a symbol of treachery and sexual transgression in her role as Cortés's lover and translator; Malinche is believed to have betrayed her own people and assisted the Spaniards in the destruction of the pre-Columbian (before European contact) world. According to Rudolfo Anaya, his role as an author is "to rescue from anonymity those familiar figures of my tradition.... *The Legend of La Llorona* [is] a novella that describes ... the trials and tribulations of the New World wailing woman, the Malinche of Mexico" ("La Llorona" 426). Anaya's two novellas reflect, therefore, his perspective on the crucial role of myth in his work (see chapter 2 in this book).

The Legend of La Llorona is Anaya's retelling of the story of an actual historical figure. According to many accounts, Malinche (as her indigenous name came to be pronounced) was a young Aztec girl from the eastern coast of Mexico, the daughter of a tribal chief born sometime around 1504. A member of the educated class, she would lose her privileged life when her father died and her mother remarried and bore a son. To clear the boy's path to power, her mother possibly sold her into slavery to Mayan traders, whose language she would soon master.

By way of background it should be recalled that the arrival of Spanish ships to Mexico in 1519—the year called "Ce Acatl" or "One Reed" in the Aztec calendar—has been considered one of the great mythic coincidences of history, as it corresponds with an Aztec prophesy: this was the very day that the god Quetzalcóatl was destined to return. "The Plumed Serpent," as he was referred to, would come from the east like the morning star, where he had lived in exile. Quetzalcóatl would return either in peace, if mankind had cared for the Earth and for one another, or in anger to punish mankind's misdeeds. Given the coincidence of their arrival date, the Spanish conquistadors were at first believed to be mythic beings. They were treated with gifts and offerings from the Aztec emperor that included slave women to carry out their daily tasks. Malinche (later baptized Marina) was among these girls.

Already proficient in several indigenous languages, Malinche quickly learned Spanish and served as the expedition's interpreter, making her a valuable asset in the Spanish conquest of the Aztec empire. She gave birth to Cortés's son in 1522, but soon after he sent for his Spanish wife and arranged for Malinche to marry his lieutenant, Juan Jaramillo. Reviled for centuries for what is considered a betrayal of her own people, Malinche's story has been reexamined and redeemed by Chicana feminists who see her as the symbolic violated mother of the Mexican people; rather than betrayer, they consider her a woman betrayed by family and culture.

Anaya's novella also reinterprets historical events, changing details of the Malinche story to suit the author's intent, which is to analyze the human motives behind the famous affair between Malinche and Cortés and the cultural impact of the encounter between the Old World and the New ("La Llorona" 426–427). *The Legend of La Llorona* is set in the mythic world of pre-Columbian society where the gods must be appeased with human sacrifices. The story traces the general lines of the historic affair between Malinche and Cortés but fuses the character of Malinche at the end with the folk figure of La Llorona: Malinche sacrifices her own sons as "warriors" of a new resistance to Spanish domination. Their young bodies are cast into a burning lake, and Malinche is transformed into the mythic wailing woman of folklore. Her terrible deed is thus given a new significance in Anaya's tale, as the Malinche/La Llorona character proclaims in the final chapter: "My sons were to be made slaves, and I paid for their liberation dearly. Now they are dead . . . but other sons of Mexico will rise against you and avenge this deed. The future will not forgive any of us" (89).

LORD OF THE DAWN: THE LEGEND OF QUETZALCÓATL

Rudolfo Anaya returned to pre-Columbian mythology in his 1987 novella, *Lord of the Dawn*, with a figure who has fascinated authors and scholars for generations: Quetzalcóatl. In David Johnson's helpful introduction to the novella, he explains the origins of the tradition revolving around the Quetzalcóatl legend, several of which are creatively combined in Anaya's novella. Quetzalcóatl is a pre-Columbian creator deity associated with the origins of the cosmos. The first half of his name, "Quetzal," is that of a rare, long-feathered bird; "coatl" means snake or serpent, and thus he is also referred to as "The Plumed Serpent." In ancient Mexican creation myths it was believed that the cosmos had undergone four cycles of creation and destruction prior to the present or fifth age; the present age is that of the "Fifth Sun" or the "Sun of Motion," so called because it "moves according to its own path" (5). (In *Jalamanta* and in other Anaya works references to the Fifth Sun are often expressed as concerns regarding the end of an age and the beginning of a new era.)

A foremost deity of the Mexican and Central American native pantheon, Quetzalcóatl is the god of the priesthood and learning, the origin of agriculture, science, and the arts. The ancient Toltec peoples of central Mexico were followers of Quetzalcóatl; kings and high priests took his name as a title. In the tenth century a cult surrounding the deity meshed with a historical figure: Quetzalcóatl was associated with a legendary Toltec ruler and priest, Ce Acatl Topiltzin Quetzalcóatl, a respected leader and spiritual model for his people. Although prosperity reigned under his rule, he was opposed by a warrior class (which resisted his objections to human sacrifice) and was eventually banished from power and exiled. Vowing to return, he journeyed east to fulfill his destiny, promising, in some accounts, to return to redeem his culture in the year Ce Acatl (1519), the date of the arrival of the Spanish ships to Mexican shores.

The Lord of the Dawn draws on mythical-historic accounts of Quetzalcóatl recorded in early documents that survived the sixteenth-century Spanish Conquest of Mexico. In these sources evil sorcerers representing the militarists in Toltec society use magic to trick Quetzalcóatl and undermine his power. After his symbolic death and resurrection, Quetzalcóatl is consumed by flames, and his heart rises to the heavens where he becomes the morning star. Anaya's novella combines various Quetzalcóatl myths with the tale of another prominent Toltec ruler, Huemac, who is jealous of Quetzalcóatl's powers and responsible for his expulsion. In *The Lord of the Dawn* Quetzalcóatl is a priest who preaches peace and advances the arts and agriculture for his people; he is devoted to poetry, song, and the ancient teachings. Following the legend, the novella ends with the promise of Quetzalcóatl's return.

Rudolfo Anaya has stated that he has found not only creative inspiration in the Quetzalcóatl myth but also important answers to contemporary problems, discovering close parallels between the present and the world of the ancient Toltecs, such as the struggle between militarists and men of peace, the materialist instincts versus spiritual thought. Toltec civilization fell due to its reliance on warfare and greed: "Even now, the story of the Toltecs and Quetzalcóatl speaks to us across the centuries, warning us to respect our deep and fragile communal relationships within nations and among nations, and our meaningful relationships to the earth" ("The Myth of Quetzalcóatl" 199).

JALAMANTA

Plot Development

Narrated in the third person, *Jalamanta* takes place in a period described as "the end of time" (5) and in a place called the "fabled Seventh City of the Fifth Sun" (2). A walled city at war with its neighbors, it is surrounded by the mud huts of its outcasts, those who had earlier revolted against the authorities. Among those outcasts are Fatimah, a goatherd, and Amado (meaning "beloved"), the man she had loved thirty years earlier who was exiled to the desert for his challenges to official control. Amado had dared to evolve his own spiritual path and was punished with banishment. The novel opens at the point at which Amado's thirty-year absence has reached an end.

During his years in exile Amado became known as "Jalamanta, he who strips away the veils that blind the soul" (3). His reputation grew as a prophet who preached of the search for "a path of illumination" to the tribes of the southern desert, a place of "suffering, death and forgetfulness" (3). Fatimah's long-awaited lover finally appears dressed all in white. She sees him at the river's edge, where Clepo the ferryman waits, surrounded by homeless people and hungry children suffering the effects of wars of destruction. Clepo does not recognize Jalamanta at first, believing him yet "another desert wanderer gone in search of the Holy Grail" (5), but Fatimah urges him to transport the stranger, sensing a familiarity that recalls her lost love. Their reunion rekindles their feelings for each other.

As Jalamanta has been weakened by his long years in the desert, Fatimah tends to his physical needs as she informs him of the changes that have occurred during his absence. A failed revolution against the "central authority" caused the deaths of many and the banishment of others. His friends Santos and Iago remain in the community outside the city; Iago is a prosperous wine merchant, and Santos is a scholar. The community learns of Jalamanta's return, and, sensing that a new age is at hand, they are eager for his preachings. Fatimah urges him to rest, however, covering him with the multicolored blanket she has woven in the tradition of the ancestors. They speak of their dreams to each other, and he grants her a simple gift—a small crystal in which is captured the energy and love of the "Universal Spirit" and the "Lords and Ladies of the Light" encountered in the desert's ancestral pyramids (12).

After several days together Jalamanta is sufficiently healed by Fatimah to "become a shepherd again" (15). He begins his daily meditations and reflects on such ideas as the healing energy of nature and the sun as "Giver of Life" (16), the unity of humanity with the cosmos, and the transcendence of the mortal body to join with the "Universal Light." Jalamanta's friends come to visit. They discuss the chaos and political repression of the central authority, a violent era that, according to Jalamanta, will give way to a new time, "the time of the Sixth Sun" (21) that will either be chaotic or peaceful, depending on mankind's creativity. Iago is cynical; less trustful of human nature than Jalamanta, he does not share his friend's optimism. As for Iago, he envies the relationship between Fatimah and Jalamanta. Having desired her for himself, he is troubled by Jalamanta's return.

In the following chapters Jalamanta meets with groups of local villagers, accompanied by Fatimah. Considering him a prophet, they pose questions to him as they search for enlightenment. In the chapter titled "The Youth Gather," Jalamanta speaks to the young, many of whom are the children of his friends, who are eager for peace after years of war and violence. He explains the meaning of his name, which is in the language of his mother's tribe, and begins to impart his ideas, many of which will be repeated in one form or another throughout the novel: that we are all a part of the universe; that our purpose in life is to strive for awareness and illumination; that we should "trust the essence within" and thus trust others to create a "community of souls" (30–31). Iago points out that Jalamanta's ideas stress a type of self-empowerment that can be interpreted as a threat to the central authority; he accuses Jalamanta of preaching revolution. "I preach a revolution of the spirit" (31) is Jalamanta's response.

Among his methods for attaining this clarity of spirit is the process of meditation, permitting the energy of nature, particularly the sun, to fill the soul. He speaks to the young of the futility of using drugs to arrive at clarity of purpose; connecting to other souls and the universal consciousness would better accomplish that goal. In subsequent chapters these concepts are repeated and expanded to include the linking of "Divine Love" or the Universal Spirit to the "First Creation" and a definition of God as the "Transcendent Other" (44). The ideas are expressed outside the framework of institutional religions: "He had no church, no cult, no following to bid to do his work" (47). The people gathered around Jalamanta share in his preachings and briefly experience an epiphany, a revealing moment of light, peace, and understanding.

When Fatimah and Jalamanta arrive home again, Fatimah decides to finally reveal her secret: she had given birth to Jalamanta's son in his absence. Unaware that he had become a father, Jalamanta had nevertheless dreamt of a young spirit by her side and now understands the meaning of those dreams. He will not see his son, however; forced to serve in the military, the young man has been reported lost in battle. Jalamanta laments his lost opportunity and regrets not having been at Fatimah's side through the ordeal.

In the chapter "Pain and Suffering" Santos and Iago discuss these topics with Jalamanta, who considers suffering an opportunity for spiritual growth. Pain and suffering are a natural part of life that can be alleviated by becoming one with the Universal Spirit. Iago, whose suffering began with his feelings of doubt, is unconvinced. He repeats the biblical message of suffering as atonement for original sin. Santos defines it differently: "Suffering is the karmic retribution for our past lives" (61). Jalamanta then describes his own suffering during his years of exile in the desert, where he met with the demons of despair, a crisis of faith brought about when he discarded the "old dogma of the moral authorities," the "old laws," to discover his own spiritual path (62).

In the desert he had tried to ease his pain in the "city of pleasure"— an orgy of temptations of drink, food, women, and distractions of every type—but that only increased his despair. The demons of despair became very real: "There in that house of darkness, they broke my bones and left me for dead. . . . The dark night of the soul came over me. I died" (63). His fragmented soul was healed by an old woman, Memoria, a shaman who was said to have the ability to fly. She served as his guide to the pathway of light, praying over him and instructing him on the way to gather together the fragments of his soul and, with the help of a community of friends, share the healing touch. Before departing, Iago warns Jalamanta of the threatening nature of his message. In the city science is preeminent, and the central authority will not take kindly to Jalamanta's alternative views. Deviation from dogma will incite the wrath of the chief inquisitor (69), but Jalamanta will not be swayed from his course.

The following morning the local people gather once again to hear Jalamanta explain the idea of the First Creation, which he describes as the coming together of energies, "imagination and consciousness struggling to become" (73). While some refer to the First Creation as God, Jalamanta prefers to use his own terms. In human souls abides a memory, he claims, and an energy that is part of the First Creation; it never dies but is transformed over time. Prior suns have lived and died, four prior ages; the present era is that of the Fifth Sun, the fifth age. The light of the sun he refers to as the "Lords and Ladies of the Light," which must enter the soul for clarity to permeate (75). When someone protests the presence of a prostitute among them as one who fails to visit the house of God, Jalamanta angrily responds: God is not housed in the great cathedrals but, rather, in the heart and in nature. All are equal. He heals the woman with his touch and tells her that she has now broken the "shell of the Self" and can "commune with the Cosmos" (77).

In the chapter "The Soul" Jalamanta explains that concept, differentiating it from the idea of the ego, which we ourselves create and which creates distances among people. Trust the instincts to return to the soul, he says. When a scholar refutes his ideas, claiming that science has destroyed the soul—"the unifying theory of physics was the only God possible" (84)—and that science must reject whatever it cannot measure, Jalamanta responds that science cannot fathom the light of love. Jalamanta strives for a clarity beyond that which the mind can grasp. The purpose of this clarity, the "ultimate quest of the soul," however, he hesitates to share at this point. "Were they ready to hear that the person on the Path of the Sun was filling the soul with light, and that was the path of becoming God?" (85).

When Jalamanta finally reveals that purpose, the elders of the village recognize it as being in keeping with the "old stories" that spoke of becoming "one with the Transcendent . . . the All Encompassing" (94). Within the crowd, however, one referred to as "Vende" (Sellout), a spy for the central authority dressed in a brown uniform with black boots who is taking notes on Jalamanta's remarks to report to the authorities, denounces Jalamanta's ideas as heresy, calling him a false prophet. Vende, Jalamanta states, is "one of us" (100), referring to the fact that he spies on his own people.

But Fatimah suggests that an even greater betrayer walks among them, their old friend Iago who knows the chief inquisitor, their childhood acquaintance: the bully Benago. Corrupted by power, Benago had exiled all of them from the city. Vende eventually delivers a letter that summons Jalamanta to meet with Benago. Their meeting takes place within the walled, deserted city. Formerly a thriving commercial and cultural center, the central authority now dedicates itself to war and the consolidation of its absolute power. There, in the "ominous tower of the citadel" (105), Jalamanta confronts the former bully of his youth.

Benago interrogates Jalamanta on his heretical beliefs, attempting to dissuade him from his course. As a representative of the central authority, Benago considers Jalamanta's ideas a threat to the status quo because they empower the people. Benago's ideas regarding religion are cynical: "Our own moral authorities promise heaven to the masses, and it gives them hope, a hope we can manipulate" (109). As a childhood acquaintance, however, he gives Jalamanta one last chance to recant his wild ideas and avoid imprisonment and torture by the generals, but Jalamanta does not fear their power. Benago allows him to leave with a final warning of the dangers that await.

Fatimah escorts him home, and there they make love for the first time after many years of separation. Meanwhile, word has spread of Jalamanta's interrogation, and a crowd gathers once again to question him. Jalamanta speaks of the meaning of death and time, reflecting on the ideas of the ancestors and those of the "old philosophies" with regard to reincarnation, as well as the practice of proper conduct: "one law serves all: Love one another" (136). When asked if he plans to establish a new church, Jalamanta explains that the Earth is his church, and its pantheon of saints are all those who have performed good works in the past, including their own ancestors, who could be called upon to guide the living toward illumination. He assists in performing a cleansing ceremony to release those past souls who have not reached the light of clarity and have attached themselves like unwelcomed ghosts to their living relatives. When asked by a young couple if their sexual passion for each other is true love, Jalamanta explains that body and spirit unite in love, which in itself reflects the Universal Spirit. Iago accuses him of condoning promiscuity, but for Jalamanta passion can lead to a higher unity of humanity.

Other topics are discussed as well, some repeating earlier ideas in the novel. Fatimah asks Jalamanta to speak of his love for the Earth, for example. Like the cosmos, he answers, the Earth possesses a soul, a spirit, a consciousness. An astronomer inquires whether mathematical rules and science provide the only knowledge of creation. For Jalamanta scientific formulas reveal the mystery of the Earth's soul and the essence of creation. A young man in the crowd who has attended with a group of natives from the area remarks that Jalamanta's teachings are similar to those of his tribal ancestors, despite the fact that Jalamanta is not of the same tribe. Such divisions among peoples, according to Jalamanta, are false; the unity that binds all has been assigned different names by different peoples, but it is the same (156).

That evening a woman comes to meet Jalamanta with a dog by her side. Kindra, whom some regard as a witch, is a shaman/healer who has helped others, including Fatimah, to cure their souls. She has discovered a way to tap the power of the animal and the natural world, the world of "guardian spirits" known to the ancestors, to counteract the effects of negative powers (159). Rejected by the moral authorities for what they consider pantheism and animal worship, Kindra is relieved that Jalamanta understands her type of healing, which is in unity with nature and the old traditions.

As the book progresses Jalamanta's fame spreads, and the crowds gathered to hear his words grow increasingly larger—city people, tribal people isolated in the hills, and even Benago's guards, who are spying on Jalamanta. The people wish to hear him speak of healing, of integrating the fragmented, traumatized spirit. According to Jalamanta a healing guide is required who will teach them to "fly" in order to recover their souls through prayer and rituals, a guide to the underworld where one can recover and restore the soul. But the soul must eventually cure itself through meditation and moments of cultivated illumination (176).

In the final chapters Jalamanta is asked if he has ever experienced doubt in his soul. He recalls his own fears and moments of crisis when he kept himself apart from others. The young daughter of a healer finally convinced him to return to the community and emerge from his "dark cave" into the light of the sun (179). His true recovery began when he was touched—healed—by unity with others. Fatimah and Jalamanta are aware that the authorities will soon apprehend him; his ideas of spiritual liberation are too threatening. His friends claim that they can protect him by hiding him if necessary. Iago offers to stand guard but betrays Jalamanta instead, realizing Fatimah's worst fears. She offers to escape with him to the desert, but they are detained as they approach Clepo's ferry. On the final pages of the novel, Jalamanta is arrested for preaching subversive ideas and taken away toward the citadel.

Themes

Jalamanta encompasses a wide variety of themes. Prominent among them are those of love and redemption. Interestingly, the format of *Ja-*

lamanta recalls that of an earlier work with similar themes that has come to be considered a minor classic: *The Prophet* by Kahlil Gibran, published in 1923. *The Prophet* combines poetic parables (simple stories with a moral) and aphorisms (short statements of truth or dogma). The narrator, separated from his homeland for many years, imparts words of wisdom to the people he lived among before his departure. Each chapter is divided into questions and answers on various topics—love, marriage, death, freedom, pain, and so forth—that will supposedly teach the seeker how to achieve mastery of life. Gibran's philosophy was fundamentally anti-authoritarian; he preached a religion of love, beauty, and redemption that became very popular in the United States in the 1960s, particularly among college students.

A similar style and philosophy is contained in *Jalamanta*. The prophetlike character answers questions that lead to teachings on trust, love, and unity with the universe. Occasionally repetitive, the work is written in a simple, poetic, and archaic tone that recalls biblical language. Although never explicitly stated, certain cultural references (among them the foods eaten by Fatimah and Jalamanta [13] and a reference to the pyramids of the ancestors in the southern desert [12]) suggest the traditional Anaya setting, the U.S. Southwest. The desert is more than just a geographic location. Metaphorically it is a reference to the barren existence of the people in need of the spiritual sustenance that an abusive central authority and a lack of spiritual guidance has created in their lives.

Jalamanta's message of unity and love stresses a communal approach to salvation (26) in which mankind transcends the material world to embrace the Earth; respect for nature is sacred. The philosophical ideas contained in *Jalamanta* recall some of the pre-Columbian notions of cosmology expressed in *Lord of the Dawn*—the end of an era, the age of the Fifth Sun (21), and the requirement to walk on the "Path of the Sun" (93), for example. *Jalamanta* does not limit itself to pre-Columbian ideas, however. Christian symbols (see "Alternative Reading" below) and Eastern mysticism also inform its outlook.

Jalamanta reflects the traditions of thought and practice associated with Buddhism and Hinduism, for example. The Buddha's enlightenment was the result of his journeying in northern India in the sixth century B.C., where he became a wandering ascetic philosopher, a seeker of truths and the correct paths to follow: Among the essential principles of Hindu belief is that of the divinity of the soul, the oneness and unity of all existence and the harmony of all religions: "Each one of us reflects the mystery of the universe" (28).

Characterization

In *Jalamanta* both plot and characters are devised as vehicles of ideas. Jalamanta, Fatimah, Iago, Santos, and Benago are not fully developed or complex characters but, rather, are allegorical types, incarnations of abstract ideas. The protagonist's original name, Amado, means "beloved," worthy of love; he explains that his new name also has a special meaning, "he who strips away the veils that blind the soul" (3). As his name implies, he is a teacher whose role is to enlighten, to demonstrate the correct path; he sacrifices his life for the truth and for others. A Christlike figure, in some ways Jalamanta also brings to mind the protagonist of Anaya's novella *The Lord of the Dawn*, Quetzalcóatl, who also paid dearly for his role in illuminating his people. The quest for enlightenment in a hero is a motif repeated throughout Anaya's works, and *Jalamanta* is no exception. The hero must experience hardships—in this case banishment and years of temptation and deprivation—in order to arrive at a place of spiritual fulfillment.

Other characters recall earlier Anaya creations as well. Fatimah (an important name in the Islamic tradition as the wife of Mohammed) is similar to other female Anaya characters. She is a gentle helpmate and healer, as well as an inspiration for the male protagonist (see the discussions of the character Ismelda from *Tortuga* in chapter 5 of this book). Iago, the envious betrayer, is similar to the earlier Anaya fictional character of Danny in *Tortuga*. A dark, shadowy figure, he is also dogmatic, inflexible, drawn inexorably to evil. (Iago's name is also a reminder of the scheming Shakespearean villian of *Othello*.) Santos (whose name means "saints") is the loyal, trustworthy friend, as his name implies; Vende is as treacherous as the translation of his name, "sellout"; and Benago represents the abusive central authority, whose lust for power leads him to betray his own people.

Finally, witches, healers, and shamans always inhabit a major part of Anaya's fictional world, and Kindra fulfills that role in *Jalamanta*. As in the case of the other characters, Kindra personifies one of the main concepts of the novel: as the healer/shaman she epitomizes the pre-Christian, pre-Columbian belief in healing mankind via an intimate relationship to nature and the animal world.

Alternative Reading: Religious/Spiritual Images

The subtitle of *Jalamanta*, *A Message from the Desert*, calls to mind the geographic origins of three major world religions. Judaism, Christianity, and Islam were born in the Middle East in similiar areas, and the wisdom of their spiritual messages has endured for centuries. The spiritual message of many of the pre-Columbian cultures of the Americas was also conceived in such regions with concepts that are in many ways unique but have points of contact with other significant traditions.

Jalamanta combines the wisdom of several religious traditions in a search for truth. It is not a religious novel per se, in that it does not look to specific religious institutions for responses to life's ultimate questions; in fact, the novel constantly speaks against dogma and organized religion, criticizing their stifling effect on creativity. Rather, *Jalamanta* confines itself to metaphysical truths found in religious traditions that house human wisdom. It looks at the larger world of spirit as part of a common humanity. In *Jalamanta* an authentic spirituality is considered an opening through which the energy of the cosmos pours into human life and prepares the way for the higher capacity of love. Anaya reveals many of these ideas in traditional religious/spiritual imagery.

A central conflict in *Jalamanta* is between good and evil, symbolized in various ways throughout the work. On one level, there is the conflict between the protagonist and the central authority. Jalamanta is a Christ-like figure whose experiences also recall those of the Toltec deity Quetzalcóatl. Banishment to the wilderness to find peace and understanding, a struggle with repressive authorities, false accusations, and betrayal by one's own people are all themes found in the Bible, but they are also elements of pre-Columbian Toltec and Aztec legends. As in the stories of Jesus Christ and Quetzalcóatl, Jalamanta must face and overcome temptations and hardships if he is to arrive at a deeper understanding of the human soul.

The language used in the novel recalls the style and tone of biblical and religious writings in general, and it is influenced by the literature of religious mysticism. The title of the chapter "The Dark Night of the Soul," for example, is a reference to a famous poem of the same name by the sixteenth-century Spanish mystic writer St. John of the Cross. He too wrote of the need for spiritual purification and contemplation on the path to divine union with God. During this process human beings may sometimes appear to be left in the shadows; the wisdom gained in the dark, hidden sources will eventually lead to the light of true glory. These dark/light contrasts also permeate *Jalamanta*: the protagonist experiences his own dark night (63) and preaches that illumination is "the soul filled with light [becoming] one with the Universal Spirit" (92).

While Hindu and Buddhist messages are relayed in the novel (see "Themes" above), most of the spiritual imagery in *Jalamanta* is from Anaya's own personal background—Christian and Native American. The end of an age of evil as a signal for the need for rebirth and change (74) is associated with the idea of an apocalypse or revelation, as found in the last book of the New Testament in the Bible, but it is also a reference to the Aztec belief in the fifth age, an era that will end in a struggle between the forces of harmony and those of violence and destruction. In Native-American traditions steps had to be taken, rites of renewal, to restore the world to its rightful condition (even today certain Native-American peoples continue to perform annual "sun dances" for world and life renewal).

Following the traditional image of Jesus Christ, a shepherd of souls, Jalamanta shares the same occupation, and his definition of proper conduct is none other than the Golden Rule: "Love one another" (136). The novel equates the quest for spiritual illumination and love with the legendary Holy Grail, a complex symbol originating in the knighthood traditions of the Middle Ages, representing, among other things, the elusive source of illumination and happiness.

Anaya's spiritual imagery does not stem from a single source, nor does it fall into a single pattern. Native-American traditions, however, the inherent passion for the Earth and its web of life, do inform many of the ideas in the novel, particularly those regarding the relationship of men and women to the cosmos, to the natural world, and to the ancestors. The beliefs that the spirits of nature and the animal world are forces that can help human beings in need (162), and that the modes of ritual healing assisted by a shaman have the power to directly perceive spirituality by placing psychic and even cosmic power at his or her disposal, are elements of the Native-American spiritual imagery that permeates *Jalamanta*.

Bibliography

Note: All page numbers in the text refer to the paperback editions of Rudolfo Anaya's novels.

WORKS BY RUDOLFO A. ANAYA

Fiction

Alburquerque. Albuquerque: University of New Mexico Press, 1992; New York: Warner Books, 1994.

Bless Me, Ultima. Berkeley, CA: Quinto Sol Publications, 1972; New York: Warner Books, 1994.

Heart of Aztlán. Berkeley, CA: Editorial Justa, 1976.

Jalamanta: A Message from the Desert. New York: Warner Books, 1996.

The Legend of La Llorona. Berkeley, CA: Tonatiuh/Quinto Sol Publications, 1984.

Lord of the Dawn: The Legend of Quetzalcóatl. Albuquerque: University of New Mexico Press, 1987.

Rio Grande Fall. New York: Warner Books, 1996.

Shaman Winter. New York: Warner Books, 1999.

The Silence of the Llano. Berkeley, CA: Tonatiuh/Quinto Sol Publications, 1982. (Short stories.)

Tortuga. Berkeley, CA: Editorial Justa, 1979; Albuquerque: University of New Mexico Press, 1995.

Zia Summer. New York: Warner Books, 1995.

Edited Collections

The Anaya Reader. New York: Warner Books, 1995. (Collection of essays, stories, and plays.)

Aztlán: Essays on the Chicano Homeland. With Francisco Lomelí. Albuquerque: University of New Mexico Press, 1991.

A Ceremony of Brotherhood, 1680–1980. With Simon J. Ortiz. Albuquerque: Academia Press, 1981. (Anthology of prose, poetry, and artwork.)

Cuentos Chicanos: A Short Story Anthology. With Antonio Márquez. Albuquerque: University of New Mexico Press, 1980.

Tierra: Contemporary Short Fiction of New Mexico. El Paso, TX: Cinco Puntos Press, 1989.

Voces: An Anthology of Nuevo Mexicano Writers. Albuquerque: El Norte Publications, 1987.

Voices from the Rio Grande. With Jim Fisher. Albuquerque: Rio Grande Writers Association Press, 1976.

Essays

"An American Chicano in King Arthur's Court." In *Old Southwest/New Southwest: Essays on a Region and Its Literature.* Ed. Judy Nolte Lensink. Tucson, AZ: Tucson Public Library, 1987: 113–118.

"Aztlán." In *The Anaya Reader.* Ed. Rudolfo A. Anaya. New York: Warner Books, 1995: 367–383.

"The Light Green Perspective: An Essay Concerning Multi-Cultural American Literature." *The Journal of the Society for the Study of the Multi-Ethnic Literature of the United States* (hereafter *MELUS*) 11, 1 (spring 1984): 27–32.

"La Llorona, El Kookoóee, and Sexuality." In *The Anaya Reader.* Ed. Rudolfo A. Anaya. New York: Warner Books, 1995: 417–428.

"Mythical Dimensions/Political Reality." In *The Anaya Reader.* Ed. Rudolfo A. Anaya. New York: Warner Books, 1995: 345–352.

"The Myth of Quetzalcóatl in a Contemporary Setting: Mythical Dimensions/Political Reality." *Western American Literature* 23, 3 (November 1988): 195–200.

"The New World Man." In *The Anaya Reader.* Ed. Rudolfo A. Anaya. New York: Warner Books, 1995: 353–365.

"*The Silence of the Llano*: Notes from the Author." *MELUS* 11, 2 (winter 1984): 47–57.

"The Writer's Landscape: Epiphany in Landscape." *Latin American Literary Review* 5, 10 (spring–summer 1977): 98–102.

"The Writer's Sense of Place: A Symposium and Commentaries." *South Dakota Review* 26, 1 (winter 1988): 93–120.

Translations

Cuentos: Tales from the Hispanic Southwest, Based on Stories Originally Collected by Juan B. Rael. Ed. José Griego y Maestas. Santa Fe: Museum of New Mexico Press, 1980.

Drama

(*Note*: All plays are as yet unpublished unless otherwise indicated.)
"Angie."
"Ay, Compadre."
Billy the Kid. In *The Anaya Reader*. Ed. Rudolfo A. Anaya. New York: Warner Books, 1995: 495–553.
"Death of a Writer."
"The Farolitos of Christmas."
"Matachines."
"The Season of La Llorona."
Who Killed Don José? In *The Anaya Reader*. Ed. Rudolfo A. Anaya. New York: Warner Books, 1995: 437–493.

Other Works

The Adventures of Juan Chicaspatas. Houston, TX: Arte Publico Press, 1985. (Epic poem.)
"Autobiography." *Contemporary Authors Autobiography Series*. Vol. 4. Detroit: Gale Research, 1986: 15–28.
A Chicano in China. Albuquerque: University of New Mexico Press, 1986. (Travel journal.)
The Farolitos of Christmas. New York: Hyperion, 1995. (Children's picture book.)
Maya's Children: The Story of La Llorona. New York: Hyperion, 1996. (Children's picture book.)

WORKS ABOUT RUDOLFO A. ANAYA

Candelaria, Cordelia. "Rudolfo Alfonso Anaya (1937–   )." In *Chicano Literature: A Reference Guide*. Ed. Julio A. Martínez and Francisco A. Lomelí. Westport, CT: Greenwood Press, 1985: 34–51.

———. "Rudolfo A. Anaya." In *Dictionary of Literary Biography: Chicano Writers*. Ed. Francisco Lomelí and Carl R. Shirley. Vol. 82. Detroit: Gale Research, 1989: 24–35.

Cantú, Roberto. "The Surname, the Corpus, and the Body in Rudolfo A. Anaya's Narrative Trilogy." In *Rudolfo A. Anaya: Focus on Criticism*. Ed. César A. González-T. La Jolla, CA: Lalo Press, 1990: 274–317.

Clark, William. "Rudolfo Anaya: 'The Chicano Worldview.'" *Publishers Weekly*, June 5, 1995: 41–42.

Colby, Vineta, ed. *World Authors, 1985–1990*. New York: H. W. Wilson Co., 1995: 10–14.

González-T., César A., ed. *Rudolfo A. Anaya: Focus on Criticism*. La Jolla, CA: Lalo Press, 1990.

Gunton, Sharon R., and Jean C. Stine, eds. "Rudolfo A(lfonso) Anaya, 1937– ." *Contemporary Literary Criticism*. Vol. 23. Detroit: Gale Research, 1983: 22–27.

Kenyon, Karen. "Visit with Rudolfo Anaya." *Confluencia* 5, 1 (fall 1989): 125–127.

Lattin, Vernon E. "Chaos and Evil in Anaya's Trilogy." In *Rudolfo A. Anaya: Focus on Criticism*. Ed. César A. González-T. La Jolla, CA: Lalo Press, 1990: 349–358.

Márquez, Teresa. "Works by and about Rudolfo A. Anaya." In *The Magic of Words: Rudolfo A. Anaya and His Writings*. Ed. Paul Vassallo. Albuquerque: University of New Mexico Press, 1982: 55–81.

Vassallo, Paul, ed. *The Magic of Words: Rudolfo A. Anaya and His Writings*. Albuquerque: University of New Mexico Press, 1982.

INTERVIEWS

Bruce-Novoa, Juan. *Chicano Authors: Inquiry by Interview*. Austin: University of Texas Press, 1980: 183–202.

Crawford, John. "Rudolfo Anaya." In *This Is About Vision: Interviews with Southwestern Writers*. Ed. William Balassi, John F. Crawford, and Annie O. Eysturoy. Albuquerque: University of New Mexico Press, 1990: 83–93.

González, Ray. "Songlines of the Southwest: An Interview with Rudolfo A. Anaya." *Bloomsbury Review* 12, 5 (September–October 1993): 3, 18.

González-T., César A. "An Interview with Rudolfo A. Anaya." In *Rudolfo A. Anaya: Focus on Criticism*. Ed. César A. González-T. La Jolla, CA: Lalo Press, 1990: 459–470.

Johnson, David, and David Apodaca. "Myth and the Writer: A Conversation with Rudolfo Anaya." In *Rudolfo A. Anaya: Focus on Criticism*. Ed. César A. González-T. La Jolla, CA: Lalo Press, 1990: 414–438.

Jussawalla, Feroza F., and Reed Way Dasenbrock, eds. *Interviews with Writers of the Post-Colonial World*. Jackson: University Press of Mississippi, 1992: 244–255.

REVIEWS AND CRITICISM

Bless Me, Ultima

Arias, Ron. Review of *Bless Me, Ultima. American Book Review* 1, 6 (March–April 1979): 8.

Booklist, December 15, 1975: 557.

Booklist, April 1, 1994: 1462.

Bruce-Novoa, Juan. "Learning to Read (and/in) Rudolfo Anaya's *Bless Me, Ultima*." In *Teaching American Ethnic Literatures*. Ed. John R. Maitino and

David R. Peck. Albuquerque: University of New Mexico Press, 1996: 179–191.

Calderon, Hector. "Rudolfo Anaya's *Bless Me, Ultima*: A Chicano Romance of the Southwest." *Critica* 1 (fall 1986): 21–47.

Cheuse, Alan. "The Voice of the Chicano: Letter from the Southwest." *The New York Times Book Review*, October 11, 1981: 15, 36–37.

Lamadrid, Enrique. "Myth as the Cognitive Process of Popular Culture in Rudolfo Anaya's *Bless Me, Ultima*: The Dialectics of Knowledge." In *Rudolfo A. Anaya: Focus on Criticism*. Ed. César A. González-T. La Jolla, CA: Lalo Press, 1990: 100–112.

Lattin, Vernon E. "The 'Horror of Darkness': Meaning and Structure in Anaya's *Bless Me, Ultima*." *Revista Chicano-Riqueña* 6, 2 (spring 1978): 51–57.

———. "The Quest for Mythic Vision in Contemporary Native American and Chicano Fiction." *American Literature* 50 (1979): 625–640.

Library Journal, February 1, 1973: 433.

Library Journal, June 1, 1994: 172.

Newkirk, Glen A. "Anaya's Archetypal Women in *Bless Me, Ultima*." *South Dakota Review* 31, 1 (spring 1993): 112–150.

New York Review of Books, March 26, 1987: 32.

Publishers Weekly, March 18, 1974: 54.

Rogers, Jane. "The Function of *La Llorona* Myth in Rudolfo Anaya's *Bless Me, Ultima*." *Latin American Literary Review* 5, 10 (spring–summer 1997): 64–69.

Testa, Daniel. "Extensive/Intensive Dimensionality in Anaya's *Bless Me, Ultima*." *Latin American Literary Review* 5, 10 (spring–summer 1977): 70–78.

Tonn, Horst. "*Bless Me, Ultima*: Fictional Response to Times of Transition." In *Rudolfo A. Anaya: Focus on Criticism*. Ed. César A. González-T. La Jolla, CA: Lalo Press, 1990: 1–12.

Wilson, Carter. "Magical Strength in the Human Heart." *Ploughshares* 4, 3 (June 1978): 190–197.

Heart of Aztlán

Albuquerque Journal, February 13, 1977: D-3.

Books of the Southwest 228 (November 1977): 1.

Bus, Heiner. "Individual Versus Collective Identity and the Idea of Leadership in Sherwood Anderson's *Marching Men* (1917) and Rudolfo Anaya's *Heart of Aztlán* (1976)." In *Rudolfo A. Anaya: Focus on Criticism*. Ed. César A. González-T. La Jolla, CA: Lalo Press, 1990: 113–131.

Gerdes, Dick. "Cultural Values in Three Novels of New Mexico." *Bilingual Review/La Revista Bilingue* 7, 3 (September–December 1980): 239–248.

Lewis, Marvin A. "Review of *Heart of Aztlán*." *Revista Chicano-Riqueña* 9, 3 (summer 1981): 74–76.

Taylor, Paul Beekman. "The Mythic Matrix of Anaya's *Heart of Aztlán*." In *On Strangeness*. Ed. Margaret Bridges. Tübingen: Narr, 1990: 201–214.

World Literature Today (spring 1979): 246.

Tortuga

Book World, May 14, 1995: 11.
Bruce-Novoa, Juan. "The Author as Communal Hero: Musil, Mann, and Anaya." In *Rudolfo A. Anaya: Focus on Criticism*. Ed. César A. González-T. La Jolla, CA: Lalo Press, 1990: 183–208.
Elias, Edward. "*Tortuga*: A Novel of Archetypal Structure." *Bilingual Review/La Revista Bilingue* 9, 1 (January–April 1982): 82–87.
Fiction International 12 (1980): 283.
Small Press Review 12 (February 1980): 8.

Alburquerque

Book World, May 14, 1995: 11.
Library Journal, July 1992: 119.
Los Angeles Times Book Review, August 30, 1992: 8.
Moran, Julio. "Anaya's Tale of *Alburquerque*: An Old Name, and the Same Old Story." *Los Angeles Times*, December 17, 1992: 5.
Nelson, Antonya. "Turf Wars in New Mexico." *The New York Times Book Review*, November 29, 1992: 22.
Publishers Weekly, May 25, 1992: 36–37.
Review of Contemporary Fiction 12, 3 (fall 1992): 201–202.
World Literature Today (winter 1994): 125.

Zia Summer

Booklist, May 15, 1995: 1610.
Book World, May 14, 1995: 5.
Kirkus Review, May 15, 1995: 669.
Publishers Weekly, April 10, 1995: 56.
Stasio, Marilyn. "Review of *Zia Summer*." *The New York Times Book Review*, July 2, 1995: 15.
World Literature Today (spring 1996): 403.

Rio Grande Fall

Barrientos, Tanya. "Rudolfo Anaya's Simmering Mystery Is a Recipe That Failed." *Chicago Tribune*, September 25, 1996: CN-3.
Booklist, September 1, 1996: 66.
Kirkus Review, July 15, 1996: 1004.
Library Journal, January 1997: 51.
Publishers Weekly, July 29, 1996: 73.
Ramos, Manuel. "New Mexico in Autumn Setting for Anaya Thriller: Characters from *Zia Summer* Brought Back." *Denver Post*, September 1, 1996: D-08.

Jalamanta: A Message from the Desert

Booklist, February 1, 1996: 915.

Kirkus Review, December 15, 1995: 1730.

Library Journal, February 1, 1996: 64.

Perera, Victor. "Parable for Our Time: *Jalamanta* Is More Spiritual Search Than Story." *Washington Post*, February 20, 1996: D-02.

Publishers Weekly, January 1, 1996: 58.

World Literature Today (autumn 1996): 957.

OTHER SECONDARY SOURCES

Augenbraum, Harold, and Margarite Fernández Olmos, eds. *The Latino Reader: An American Literary Tradition from 1542 to the Present.* Boston: Houghton Mifflin Co., 1997.

Bruce-Novoa, Juan. *Retrospace: Collected Essays on Chicano Literature.* Houston, TX: Arte Publico Press, 1990.

Gonzalez-Berry, Erlinda, ed. *Pasó por aquí: Critical Essays on the New Mexican Literary Tradition, 1542–1988.* Albuquerque: University of New Mexico Press, 1989.

Lattin, Vernon E., ed. *Contemporary Chicano Fiction: A Critical Survey.* Binghamton, NY: Bilingual Press, 1986.

Saldívar, Ramón. *Chicano Narrative: The Dialectics of Difference.* Madison: University of Wisconsin Press, 1990.

Showalter, Elaine. "The Feminist Critical Revolution." In *The New Feminist Criticism: Essays on Women, Literature, and Theory.* Ed. Elaine Showalter. New York: Pantheon Books, 1985.

Sommers, Joseph, and Tomás Ybarra-Frausto, eds. *Modern Chicano Writers: A Collection of Critical Essays.* Englewood Cliffs, NJ: Prentice-Hall, 1979.

Tatum, Charles. *Chicano Literature.* Boston: Twayne Publishers, 1982.

Index

About the Author

MARGARITE FERNÁNDEZ OLMOS is Professor of Modern Languages and Literatures at Brooklyn College of the City University of New York, where she teaches courses in Spanish and Latin American Studies. She has authored and coedited numerous volumes including *The Latino Reader: An American Literary Tradition from 1542 to the Present* (1997) and *Remaking a Lost Harmony: Short Stories from the Hispanic Caribbean* (1995), for which she was coeditor and translator, and has written a wealth of articles for both Spanish- and English-language journals.